Origami,
Plain and Simple

Models by Robert Neale
Text and Graphics by Thomas Hull

Photographs by Lionel Delevingne

St. Martin's Press
New York

Library of Congress Cataloging-in-Publication Data

736.982
NEA

Neale, Robert E.
    Origami, plain and simple / Robert Neale and Thomas Hull.
      p.   cm.
    ISBN 0-312-10516-9 (pbk.)
    1. Origami.   I. Hull, Thomas.   II. Title.
TT870.N4 1994
736'.982—dc20

93-44067
CIP

First Edition: April 1994
10 9 8 7 6 5 4 3 2 1

Contents

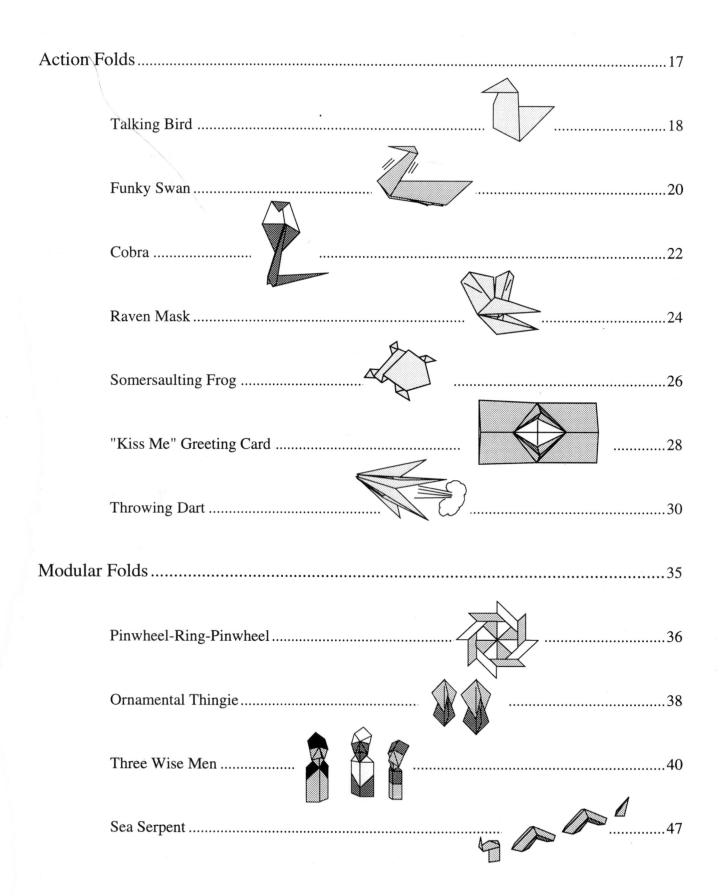

Introduction

Hello. I'm the author of this book but not the creator of the origami models inside. That credit goes to Robert Neale, origamist extraordinaire.

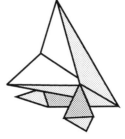

Bob Neale began folding paper in 1958 and quickly became involved with the budding family of origamists in New York City. This is when he first met the late Lillian Oppenheimer, whom he calls (as do many others) his "paperfolding grandmother." Folding sessions were held in Lillian's apartment for years and years. In the early 80s, the group bloomed into what is now known as The Friends of The Origami Center of America, of which Bob was the president for a few years. Throughout all this time Bob was folding and teaching folds. In fact, some of his paper creations were appreciated enough to find their way into various origami anthologies. Eventually Bob left New York, but he continued to fold, fold, fold.

By the time I first met Bob in 1988, the origami world had seen much change. The Friends had over a thousand members, and the emergence of origami techno-gods like John Montroll and Robert Lang added amazing levels of complexity and detail to the art. Yet even in the midst of this apparent "golden age" of origami, Bob Neale had yet to publish a book of his own folds. This fact was all the more surprising to me when I was allowed to explore the boxes and boxes of original origami models that he had hidden in his attic. It seemed an outright crime that none of these elegant folds had made it to the printed page. Indeed, I learned that Bob had been inventing enough modular origami folds during the late 60s to rival the work of Tomoko Fuse, whose excellent books (circa 1982) have made her the queen of modular folding. Indeed, while the general trend in origami had been toward greater and greater complexity, Bob had developed hundreds of simple folds, each a wonder of economy and elegance. Indeed, why didn't he publish any of these folds?

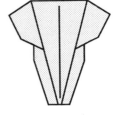

Well, one thing that Bob Neale hates to do is diagram origami folds, and that's where I came in.

This is a book of simple-to-intermediate folds. The goal in designing the book was to provide diagrams that were intuitively clear, as opposed to relying on an origami vocabulary to describe each step.

The reason for this attitude is simple. When trying to learn origami from a book, the reader is really learning two things at the same time: 1) how to fold paper and 2) how to read origami diagrams. These are two distinct skills, and their combined effect can be discouraging, to say the least.

Thus, we have tried to eliminate as much origami terminology as possible from the text. The only lingo required for this book is a complete understanding of the meaning of the word "fold." Some standard origami symbols are used, but these are more self-descriptive. However, a symbol key is included in the back of the book as a reference.

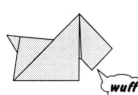

The models get progressively more difficult as you thumb your way through the book. The first two sections, Simple Folds and Action Folds, contain the easiest models; try these first. Definitely do not attempt complicated folds like "Frog with a Big Mouth, Tongue, and Eyes" or "Elephant Major" without practicing the simpler folds. We hope our efforts will be satisfactory to the beginning as well as more advanced folder. Enjoy!

—Thomas Hull
Wakefield, RI 1994

Folding Tips

Tip 1 There are two basic types of folds, and two types of dotted lines to describe them:

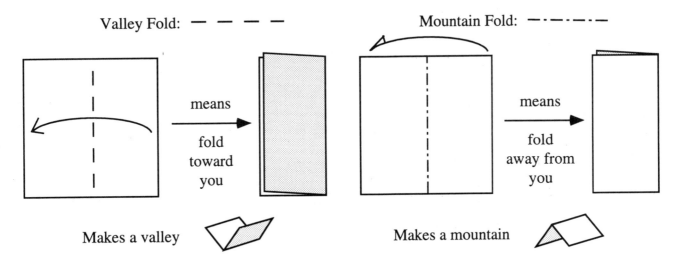

Valley Fold: — — — —   Mountain Fold: —·—·—·—

means
fold toward you

means
fold away from you

Makes a valley   Makes a mountain

With just an understanding of the difference between the mountain and valley folds, you should be able to tackle the models in this book with confidence. However, a list of symbols is provided at the end of the book for those who want to know more about the diagrams.

Tip 2 Be assertive! **Crease firmly.**
Wimpy creases can result in vague and ambiguous models.

What am I?

Tip 3 Don't get in over your head!
Start with the **simple** models and work your way up.

Tip 4 Look before you leap!

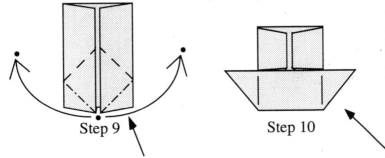

Step 9   Step 10

When working on a certain step, look ahead at the next step to see what the result is supposed to look like.

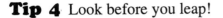

If **this** doesn't make sense, try looking at **this**.

On Paper

Most people do origami with special origami paper that is square and colored on one side and white on the other. People like origami paper because it folds well and comes in all sorts of wild colors. Such paper can usually be found in bookstores, art supply stores, or can be ordered from the organizations listed below.

The diagrams in this book assume that such paper is being used; the pictures show the white side of the paper as white, and the colored side as gray. Some of the models, like the Owlet and the inhabitants of the Frog Pond, use the white side of the paper for visual effects (to make eyes and such).

However, all that is really required to make these models is a square. Use construction paper, notebook paper, junk mail, magazine covers, napkins, rugs, or use your imagination!

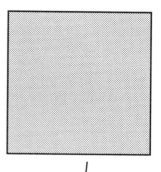

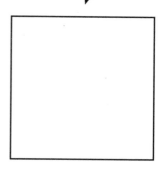

Origami Information

For those who would like to know more about the art of origami, the two major American and British origami societies are listed. Both publish newsletters, organize origami conventions, run mail-order supply centers, and are highly recommended.

The Friends of The Origami Center of America
Box RN-1
15 West 77th Street
New York, NY 10024
USA

The British Origami Society
#11 Yarningale Road
Kings Heath
Birmingham, B14 6LT
England

Simple Folds

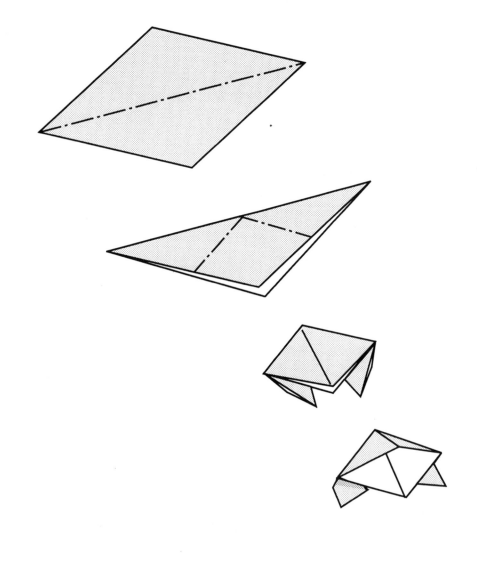

Frog with a Big Mouth

This wonderfully simple fold captures an unmistakably "froggy" personality — just two legs and a big mouth!

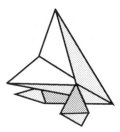

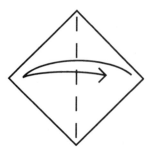

1) White side up. Fold in half along a diagonal and open again.

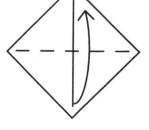

2) Fold the other diagonal.

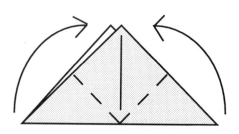

3) (Enlarged view) Fold the corners to the top.

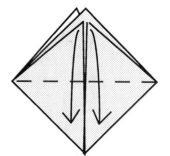

4) Fold the two points down.

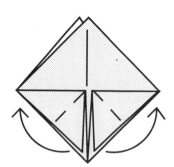

5) Fold the two points to the sides.

the mouth

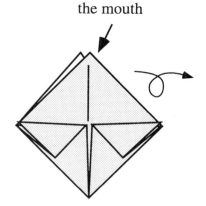

6) Open the mouth, turn over, and you're done!

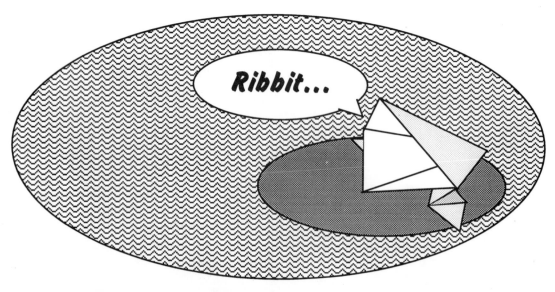

Ribbit...

6

Holy Shield

In this model, the center cross can be made as big, or as small, as you like. Just modify the folds in step 3!

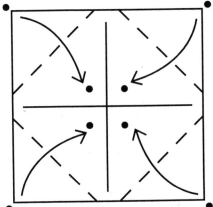

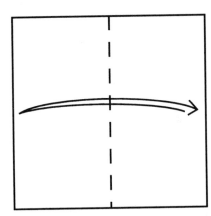

1) White side up. Fold and unfold from side to side.

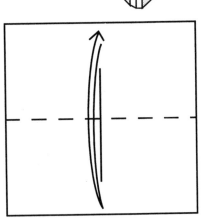

2) Repeat in the other direction.

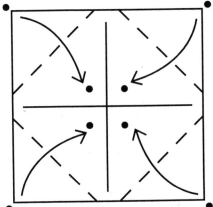

3) Fold all four corners towards the center, **but not all the way!**

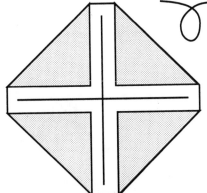

4) Be sure to make the gaps even. Turn over.

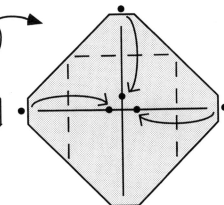

5) Now fold three flaps to the center...

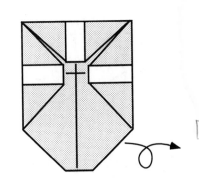

6) ... like this. Turn over, and you're done!

7) The completed holy shield.

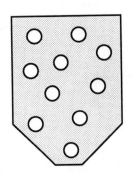

The traditional Japanese holy shield used hole-cutting techniques which modern paperfolders frown upon.

Owlet and Family

Some of the steps in this model (specifically, steps 2, 4, and 8) may be done "to taste," giving individual character to each owl and owlet. These owls were inspired by the ideas of the famous Japanese paperfolder Akira Yoshizawa.

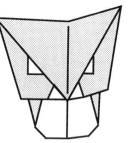

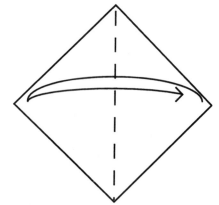

1) White side up. Fold and unfold along the diagonal.

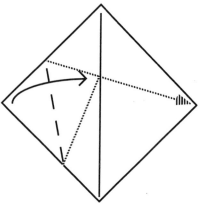

2) Fold the left corner to the center line, but aim the top edge so that it "shoots" the right corner...

3) ...like this. Fold the right corner to the left.

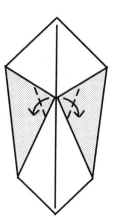

4) Fold the corners outward. (You're making the eyes!)

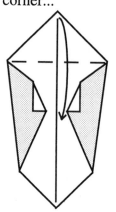

5) Fold the top point down.

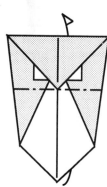

6) Fold the bottom point behind.

7) Turn over.

8) Fold the top point down to taste.

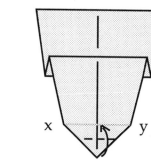

9) Fold the bottom point up to the x-y line.

8

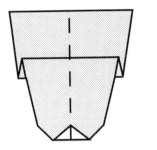

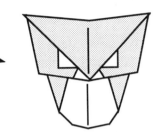

10) Crease the middle. (This will let the owl stand up.)

11) Turn over, and you're done!

Owlet

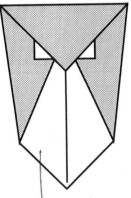

1) Using a smaller square, follow steps 1-4 of the Owl.

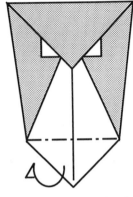

2) Fold the bottom point behind.

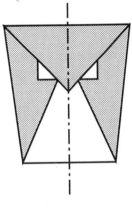

3) Emphasize the vertical crease, and the Owlet is done!

9

Simple Fish

Don't let all the "pre-creases" in steps 1-4 scare you!
They actually make the rest of the folding much easier.

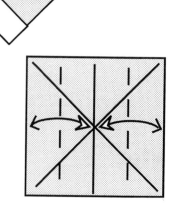

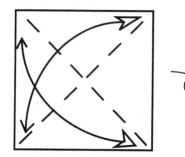

1) White side up. Fold and
unfold along both diagonals.
Turn over.

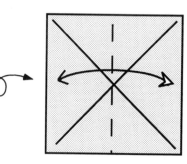

2) Fold and unfold.

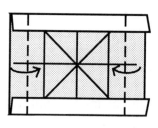

3) Fold the sides to the center
line and unfold.

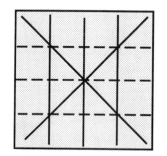

4) Repeat steps 2 and 3 in the
other direction.

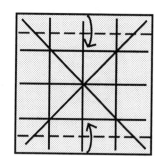

5) Fold the top and bottom
edges to the closest line.

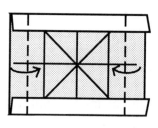

6) Repeat step 5 with the left
and right edges.

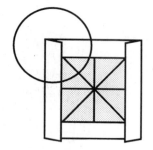

7) Zoom in on the upper left
corner.

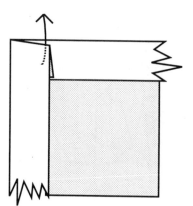

8) Now pull out the original
corner of the paper...

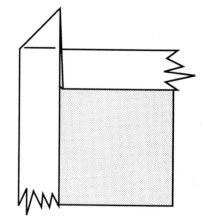

9) ...like this. Zoom out.

10

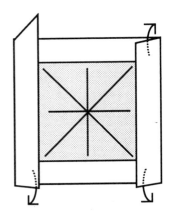

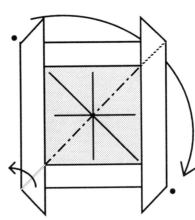

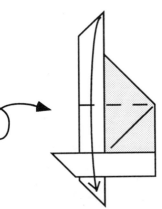

10) Repeat steps 8 and 9 on the other three corners.

11) Fold along one of the diagonals **away from you**.

12) Fold along the existing crease.

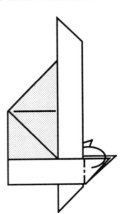

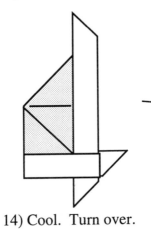

13) Now tuck the small triangle behind the two layers underneath.

14) Cool. Turn over.

15) Repeat steps 12-14 on the other flap.

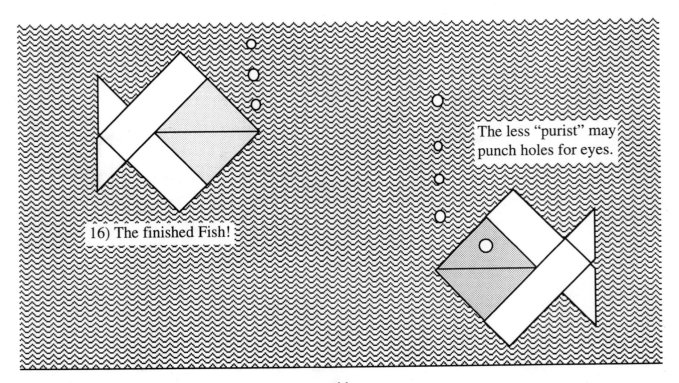

16) The finished Fish!

The less "purist" may punch holes for eyes.

Simple Wallet

A square with side length 9-10 inches will produce a wallet that can hold business and credit cards.

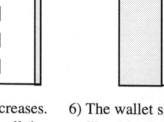

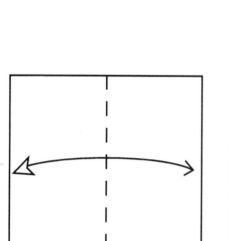

1) White side up. Fold and unfold from side to side.

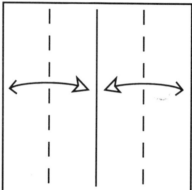

2) Fold and unfold the left and right sides to the center.

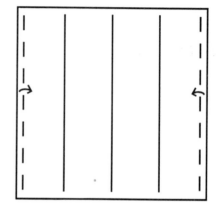

3) Then fold about a quarter-inch in on the left and right sides.

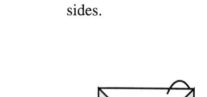

4) Fold the two top corners to the 1/4 creases as shown.

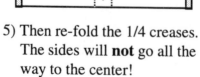

5) Then re-fold the 1/4 creases. The sides will **not** go all the way to the center!

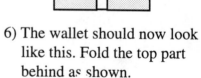

6) The wallet should now look like this. Fold the top part behind as shown.

12

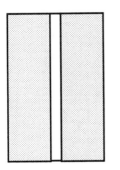

7) OK! Turn over.

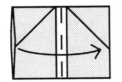

8) Fold the bottom edge to the top.

9) Now tuck this flap into the pockets underneath. This will create some pockets for the wallet.

10) Close the wallet up...

11) ... and you're done!

Many wallet variations can be made. Try your hand at the one on the right!

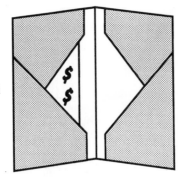

Elephantis Abstractum

This model showcases a new minimalist style of folding that has won Bob Neale's interest. It represents a careful study of form, elegance, and simplicity!

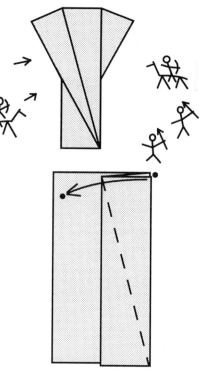

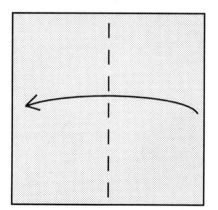

1) Colored side up. Fold the right edge to the left.

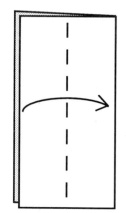

2) Then fold one layer to the right edge.

3) Make the diagonal crease as shown, bringing **one layer only** to the left...

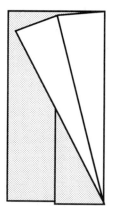

4) ...like this. Turn over.

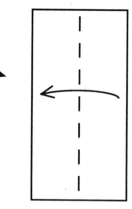

5) Fold **one layer** of paper to the left.

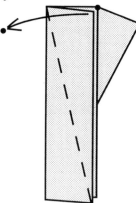

6) This is similar to step 3. Be sure to look ahead to see what this move is supposed to look like!

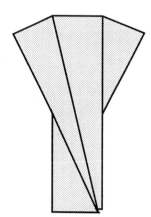

7) The Abstract Elephant! Stand it on your coffee table, and watch the opinions fly!

Scottie Dog

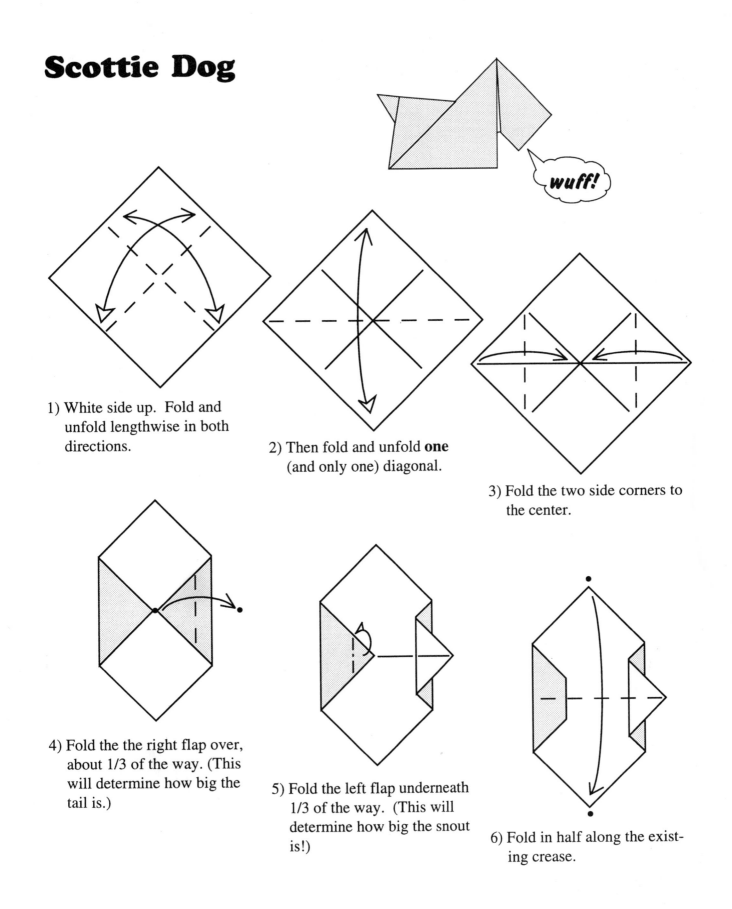

1) White side up. Fold and unfold lengthwise in both directions.

2) Then fold and unfold **one** (and only one) diagonal.

3) Fold the two side corners to the center.

4) Fold the the right flap over, about 1/3 of the way. (This will determine how big the tail is.)

5) Fold the left flap underneath 1/3 of the way. (This will determine how big the snout is!)

6) Fold in half along the existing crease.

wuff!

15

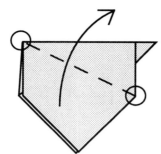 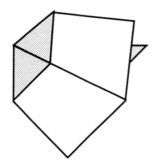 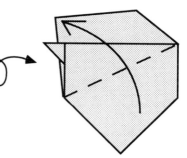

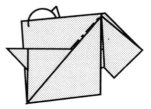

7) Careful here! Fold **one layer** up using the two corners shown as guides.

8) Like this! Turn over.

9) Repeat step 7 on this side.

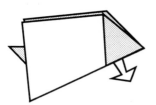 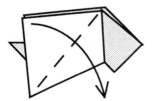

10) Now slide your finger underneath and pull out some paper...

11) ...like this! Fold the white flap down to meet the dog's head.

12) Wow! Repeat step 11 behind.

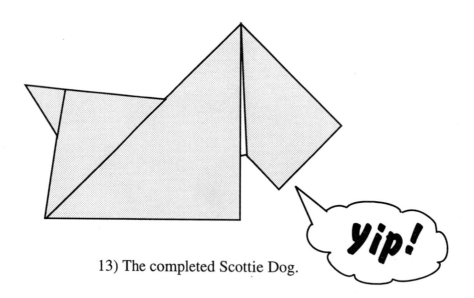

13) The completed Scottie Dog.

yip!

Action Folds

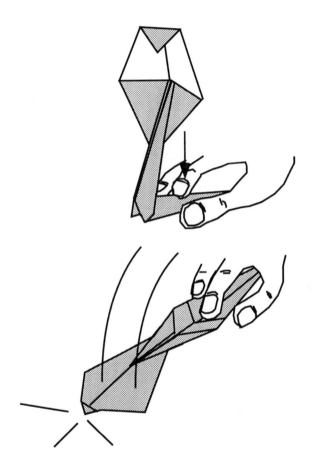

These folds incorporate mechanisms that allow you to perform an "action" with them.

Talking Bird

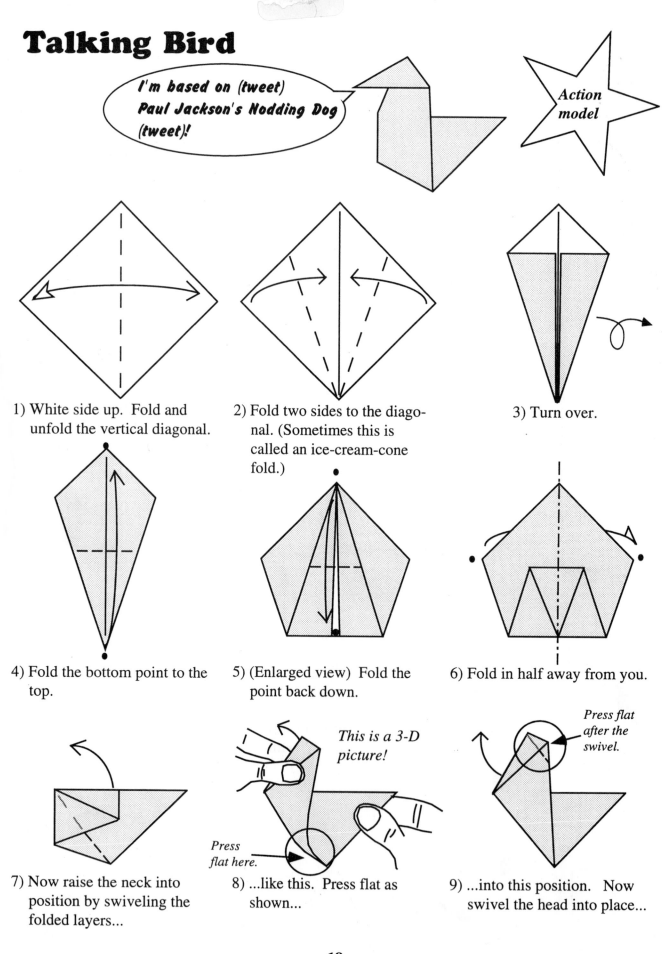

I'm based on (tweet) Paul Jackson's Nodding Dog (tweet)!

Action model

1) White side up. Fold and unfold the vertical diagonal.

2) Fold two sides to the diagonal. (Sometimes this is called an ice-cream-cone fold.)

3) Turn over.

4) Fold the bottom point to the top.

5) (Enlarged view) Fold the point back down.

6) Fold in half away from you.

7) Now raise the neck into position by swiveling the folded layers...

8) ...like this. Press flat as shown...

This is a 3-D picture!

Press flat here.

9) ...into this position. Now swivel the head into place...

Press flat after the swivel.

18

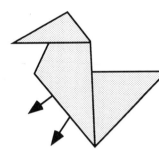 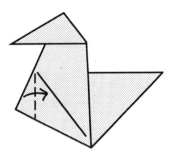 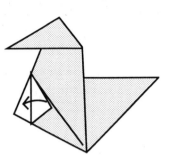

10) ...like this. Pull out two loose flaps from inside the model.

11) Fold the **top layer only**, using the existing crease as a guide.

12) Undo step 11.

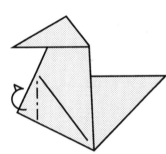 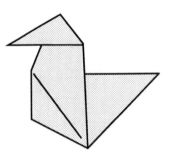

13) Now, using the crease just made, fold the flap inside the bird.

14) Fold the other flap inside to meet the first one.

15) The Talking Bird completed!

To make the bird talk

Hold as shown, and pull the tail gently.

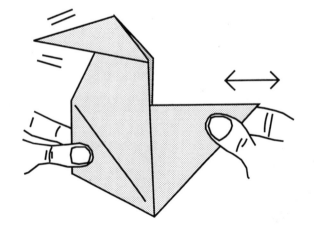

Funky Swan

A variation of the traditional swan, this model moves its head back and forth in a truly funky way!

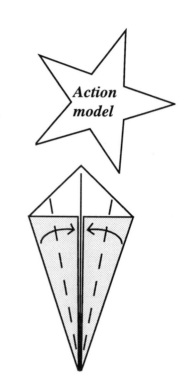

Action model

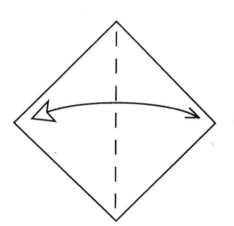

1) White side up. Fold and unfold the vertical diagonal.

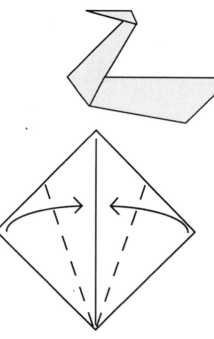

2) Fold two sides to the diagonal.

3) Fold to the diagonal again!

4) Turn over.

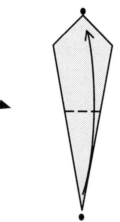

5) Fold the bottom point to the top.

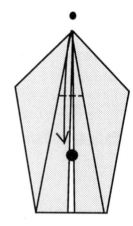

6) (Enlarged view) Fold the point approximately 1/3 of the way down.

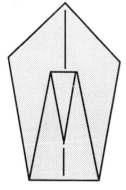

7) Turn over.

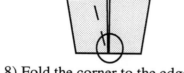

8) Fold the corner to the edge...

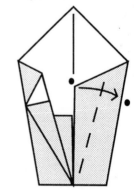

9) ...like this. Repeat on the right.

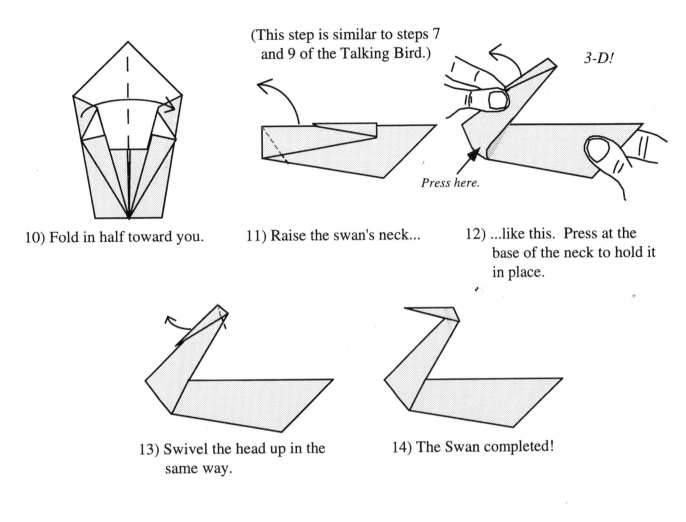

(This step is similar to steps 7 and 9 of the Talking Bird.)

3-D!

Press here.

10) Fold in half toward you.

11) Raise the swan's neck...

12) ...like this. Press at the base of the neck to hold it in place.

13) Swivel the head up in the same way.

14) The Swan completed!

To activate the funk

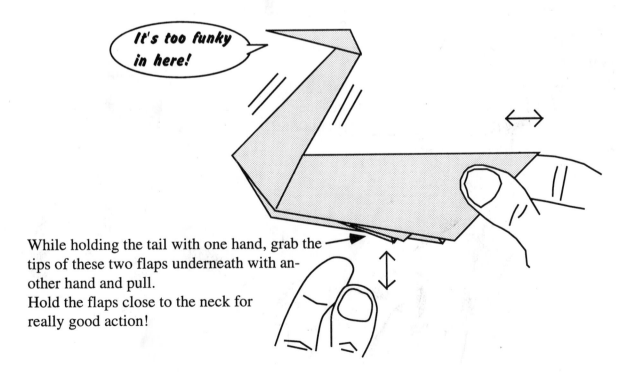

It's too funky in here!

While holding the tail with one hand, grab the tips of these two flaps underneath with another hand and pull.
Hold the flaps close to the neck for really good action!

Cobra

This cobra is a real gem of a fold, but it has some tricky steps. Be persistent, and follow the directions carefully! The model was inspired by Paul Jackson's "Pecking Bird."

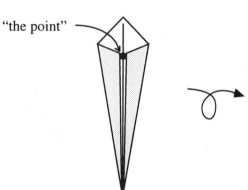

sssssssss

Action model

1) Follow steps 1-4 of the Funky Swan (page 20). Locate the point where the folded edges meet the center line and call this "the point."

"the point"

2) Turn over, and fold the bottom tip to "the point" of step 1 fame.

3) Fold in half away from you.

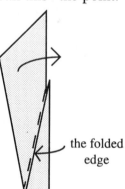

the folded edge

4) Fold one layer to the right, making a crease along the folded edge. **The model will not lie flat!**

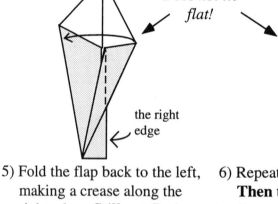

Does not lie flat!

the right edge

5) Fold the flap back to the left, making a crease along the right edge. **Still not flat!**

6) Repeat steps 4 & 5 behind. **Then** the model should lie flat.

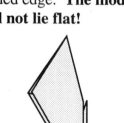

7) Pull the flap from step 2 out and over the other layers.

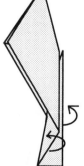

8) View from the bottom...

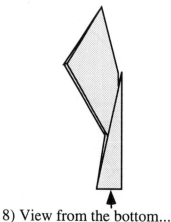

9) ...and turn the corner inside out (be assertive now)...

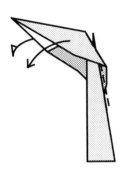 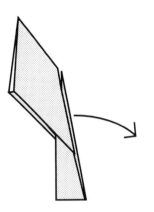 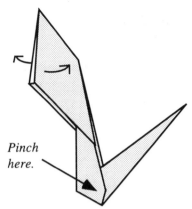

10) ...to look like this (normal view, does **not** lie flat). Bring the flaps together to the left...

11) ...to look like this. Swing the tail out to look cobra-ish.

12) Pinch the body to hold the tail in place. Open the head and look from the front.

Pinch here.

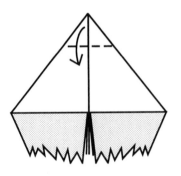 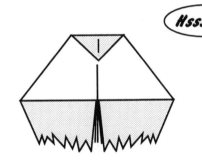 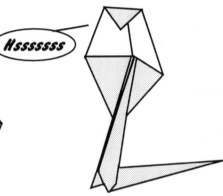

Hsssssss

13) Close-up of the head. Fold the tip down a little.

14) Like this. Are you scared yet?

15) You should be!

To make the Cobra strike

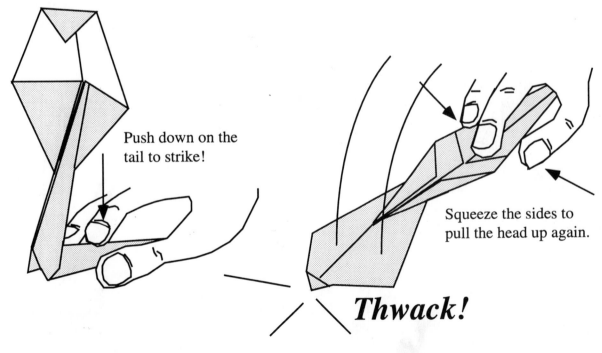

Push down on the tail to strike!

Squeeze the sides to pull the head up again.

Thwack!

Raven Mask

This mask works like a puppet.
Get ready to fulfill all your ventriloquist fantasies!

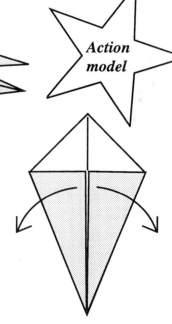

Action model

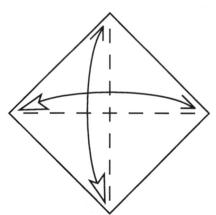

1) White side up. Fold and unfold both diagonals.

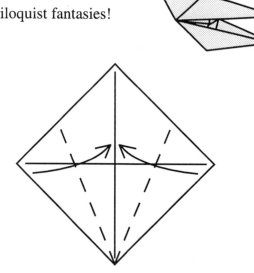

2) Bring two sides to the center line...

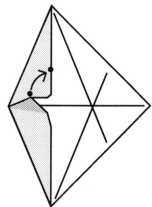

3) ...like this. Then undo step 2.

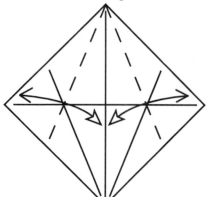

4) Repeat steps 2-3 with the other half of the paper.

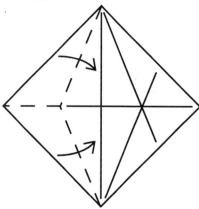

5) Now we have a bunch of creases. Fold the two on the left half at the same time...

6) ...like this. Let the short flap point up (i.e., press it flat).

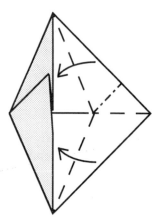

7) Repeat steps 5-6 on the right.

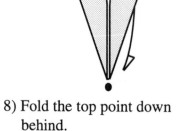

8) Fold the top point down behind.

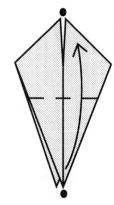

9) (Enlarged view) Fold one layer up to the top.

24

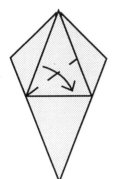

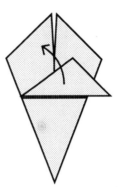

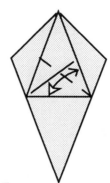

10) Then fold the left edge of this flap down to the middle line...

11) ...like this. Bring the flap back up.

12) Repeat steps 10-11 in the other direction.

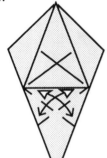

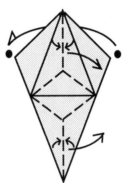

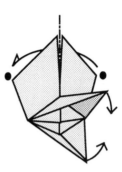

13) Repeat steps 10-12 on the lower flap.

14) OK. We're doing several things at once here. Form the beak with the two flaps while bringing the back sides together...

15) ...Step 14 in progress. Bring the back sides all the way together...

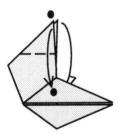

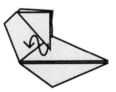

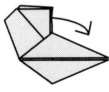

16) ...like this! Fold one of the head flaps down below the beak-line. **Repeat behind.**

17) Now tuck the end of this flap behind the beak. **Repeat behind.**

18) Cool! Open the back and you're done!

To make the Raven talk

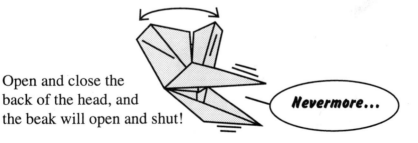

Open and close the back of the head, and the beak will open and shut!

Nevermore...

Can you figure out how to add eyes to the Raven?

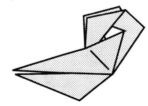

Somersaulting Frog!

This is a simple variation of the classic jumping frog. Bob added legs and the ability to do a midair "flip" as it jumps!

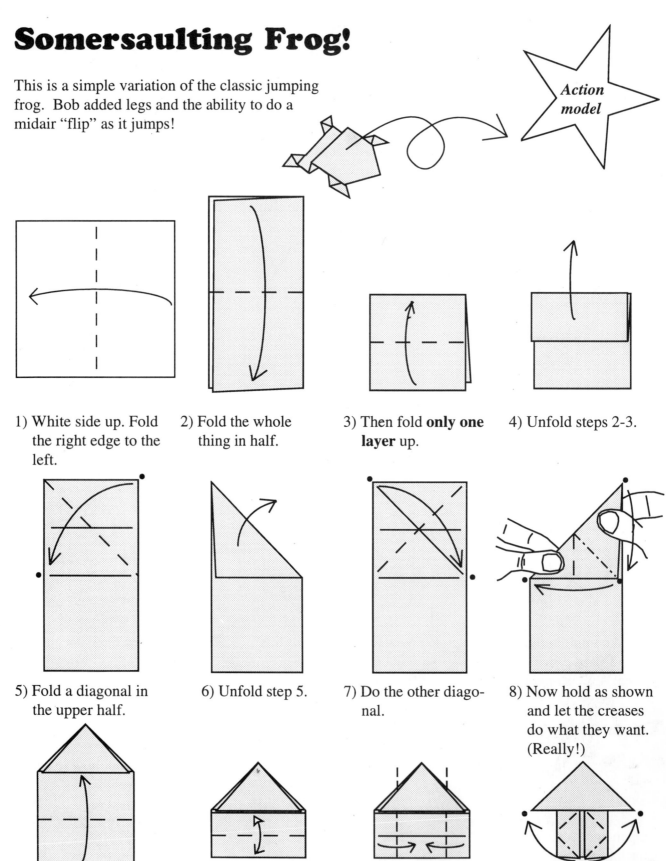

Action model

1) White side up. Fold the right edge to the left.

2) Fold the whole thing in half.

3) Then fold **only one layer** up.

4) Unfold steps 2-3.

5) Fold a diagonal in the upper half.

6) Unfold step 5.

7) Do the other diagonal.

8) Now hold as shown and let the creases do what they want. (Really!)

9) It should look like this. Fold the bottom edge up.

10) Fold the bottom edge up again, but this time unfold.

11) Bring the sides together, under the triangle.

12) Spread the two bottom flaps apart, so it looks...

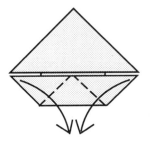

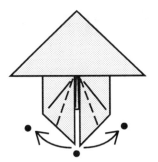

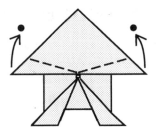

13) ...like this! Make diagonal creases to bring the flaps down.

14) The paper will feel thick, but fold the center edges of the flaps to the crease line...

15) ...like this. Then make arms...

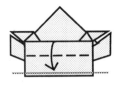

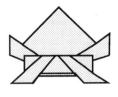

16) ...yeah. Fold the lower half up (use the existing crease).

17) OK. ·Now the paper will be very thick. Persist, though, by folding the feet down so that the "feet edge" **almost meets** the folded edge...

18) ...like this. Coolness! Turn over and you're all done.

To activate the jump

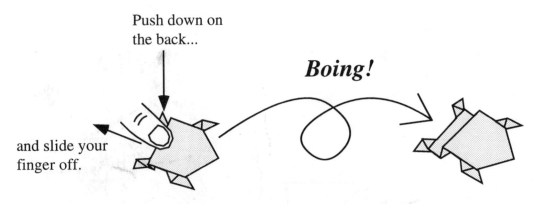

Push down on the back...

Boing!

and slide your finger off.

You can also make the Somersaulting Frog with a dollar bill or a 3x5 index card. Try it!

"Kiss Me" Greeting Card

The beginning origamist quickly learns how well-suited origami is for various holiday gifts—on Valentine's Day, for example!

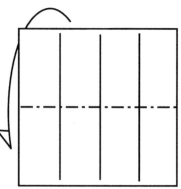

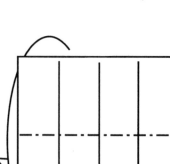

Action model

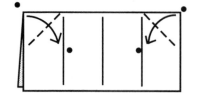

1) White side up. Fold and unfold from side to side.

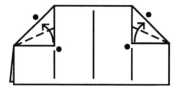

2) Fold the sides to the center and unfold.

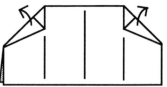

3) Fold in half away from you.

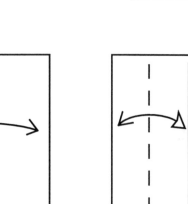

4) Fold both top corners to the center as shown.

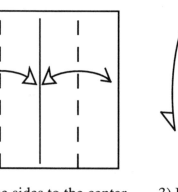

5) Fold the bottom edges of these flaps to the folded edge.

6) Undo steps 4 and 5.

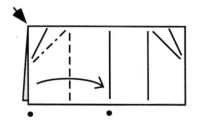

7) Squash the upper left corner while folding the lower left edge to the center line.

8) Zoom in on the left.

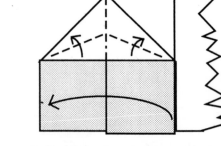

9) Fold the flap back to the left, but at the same time lift the white edges up. **Use existing creases!**

28

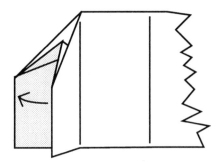

10) Step 9 in progress...

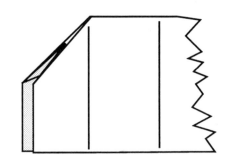

11) ...like this. **Repeat** steps 7-10 on the right.

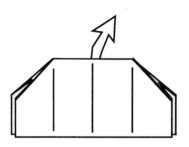

12) Normal view. Now open the model completely!

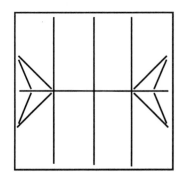

13) White side up. Rotate 90 degrees.

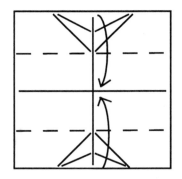

14) Fold the top and bottom to the center, using existing creases.

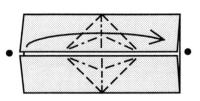

15) Fold in half while allowing the creases from step 9 and 11 to take shape.
Then you're done!

To activate the kiss

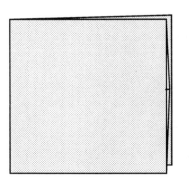

Just open!

Smack!

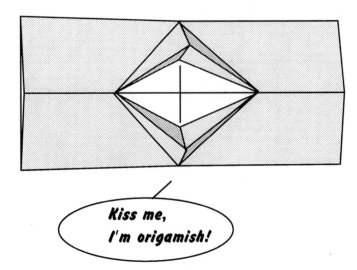

Kiss me, I'm origamish!

29

Throwing Dart

Although slightly more advanced, this fold really flies!

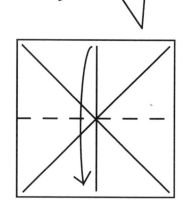

Action model

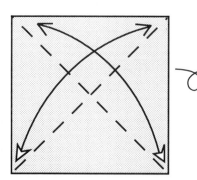

1) Colored side up. Fold and unfold both diagonals. Then turn over.

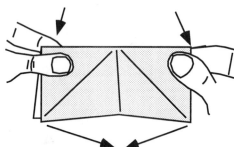

2) Fold and unfold from side to side.

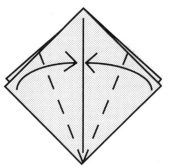

3) Fold the top side to the bottom.

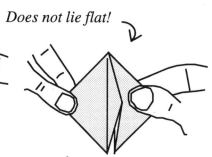

Does not lie flat!

4) Pinch the two top corners and swing the bottom corners together...

5) ...like this. Flatten by swinging a flap to the left and a flap to the right.

6) (Enlarged view) Fold the lower left and right edges to the center line.

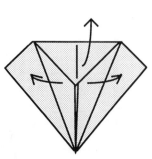

7) Fold the top point down as shown.

8) Unfold steps 6 and 7.

Use this crease.

9) Lift **one layer** of paper up. Use the crease from step 7!

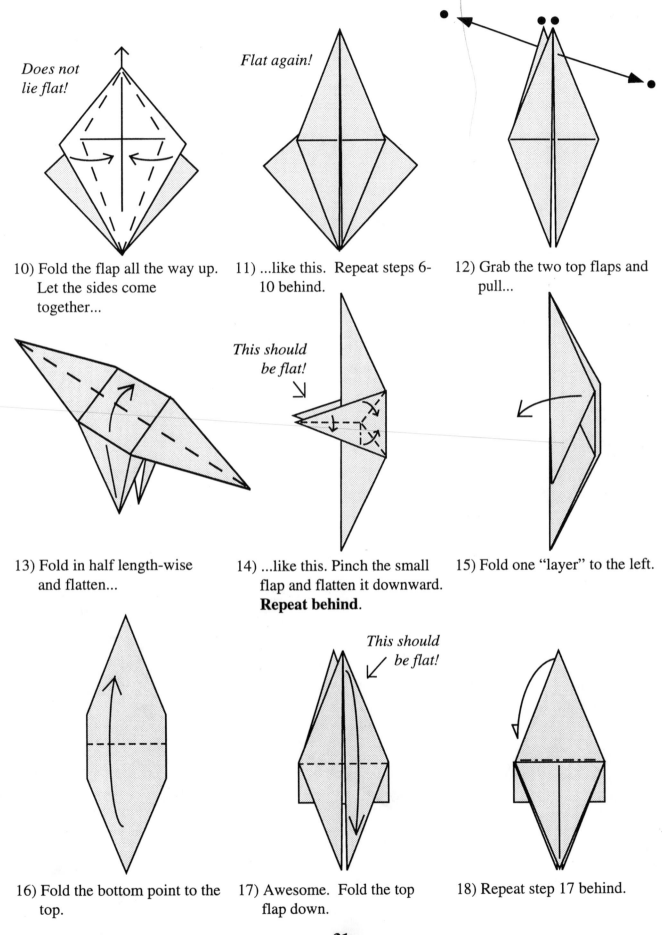

Does not lie flat!

Flat again!

10) Fold the flap all the way up. Let the sides come together...

11) ...like this. Repeat steps 6-10 behind.

12) Grab the two top flaps and pull...

13) Fold in half length-wise and flatten...

This should be flat!

14) ...like this. Pinch the small flap and flatten it downward. **Repeat behind.**

15) Fold one "layer" to the left.

16) Fold the bottom point to the top.

This should be flat!

17) Awesome. Fold the top flap down.

18) Repeat step 17 behind.

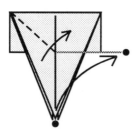

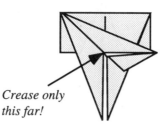
Crease only this far!

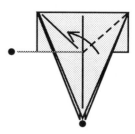

19) Now fold one layer to the right, **but do not crease all the way** (see the next step).

20) Crease only as far as the center line. Then unfold step 19.

21) Repeat steps 19-20 on the right.

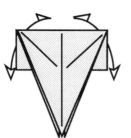

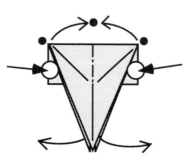

3-D picture!

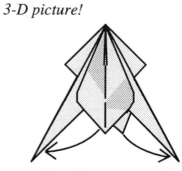

22) Repeat steps 19-21 behind.

23) Pinch the sides and swing the top corners together...

24) ...like this! Make the model flat by swinging the flaps to the left and right.

Flat again!

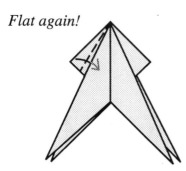

Pinch firmly here.

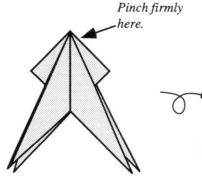

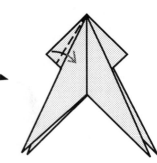

25) Fold **one** top flap inside the model.

26) Press firmly on the dart's "head." Then turn over.

27) Repeat step 25.

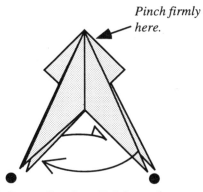 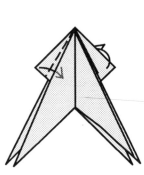 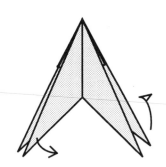

28) Press firmly. Fold one leg to the left. Repeat behind.

29) Then repeat steps 25-27.

30) Make the legs perpendicular to each other, and you're done!

To throw the Dart

Hold the Dart under the nose between thumb and forefinger. Then give it a good throw.

The layers of paper at the Dart's head make it correctly weighted for flight!

WARNING: When made well, the Dart's nose can be quite sharp. Use discretion when throwing the Dart at people.

Modular Folds

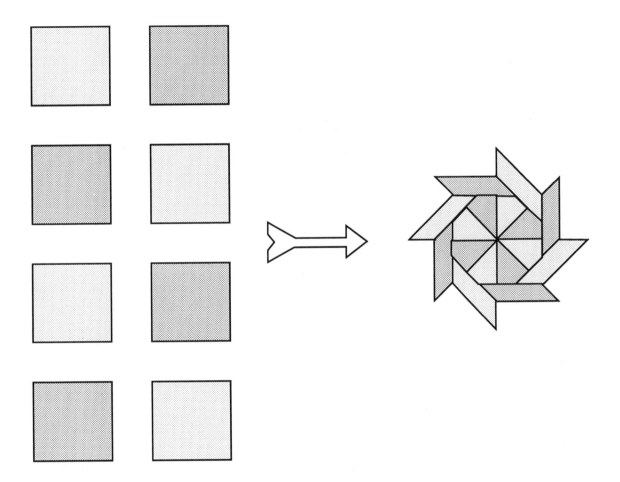

The models in this section require folding more than one sheet
of paper and joining them together to make the final object.

Pinwheel-Ring-Pinwheel

In this modular fold, we make eight identical "units" and then link them together without glue to produce a Pinwheel that can be transformed into a Ring!

To make a unit

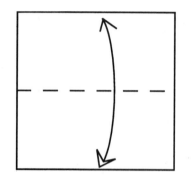

1) White side up. Fold and unfold.

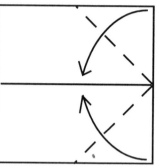

2) Fold the two right-hand corners to the center line.

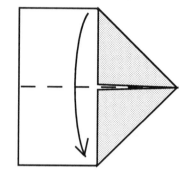

3) Fold in half!

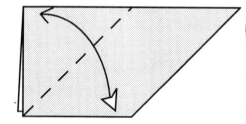

4) (Enlarged view) Fold the upper left corner down and unfold.

5) Reverse the upper left corner inside the model...

6) ...like this. The module is done! Make 8 of 'em.

To link 'em together

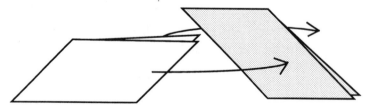

Make these flaps "hug" the other module.

1) Bring the flaps of one piece around another as shown.

2) Then tuck the excess flaps around the other module so that they hug it tightly!

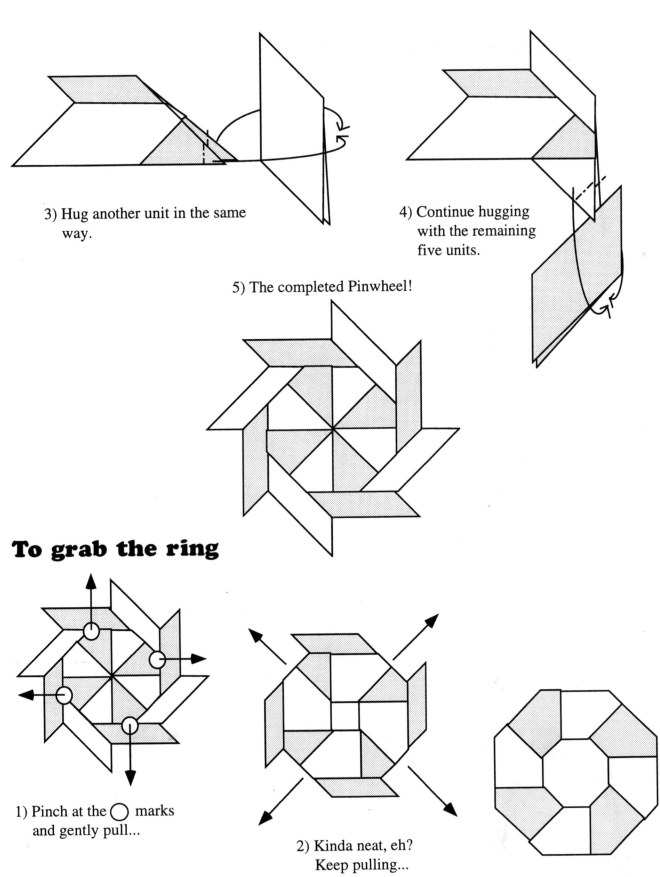

3) Hug another unit in the same way.

4) Continue hugging with the remaining five units.

5) The completed Pinwheel!

To grab the ring

1) Pinch at the ○ marks and gently pull...

2) Kinda neat, eh? Keep pulling...

3) ...and end up with a Ring!

Ornamental Thingie

Origami tends to hang very well, as this model shows. Hang one from your chandelier or, better yet, make a pair of earrings out of them!
This model was independently discovered by Brenda Rivera and Robert Neale.

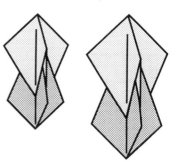

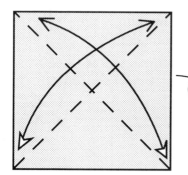

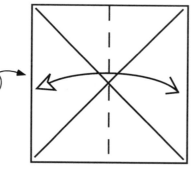

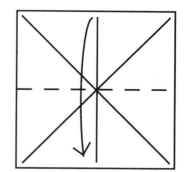

1) Colored side up. Fold and unfold both diagonals and turn over.

2) Fold from side to side and unfold.

3) Fold the top edge to the bottom.

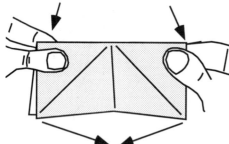

Does not lie flat!

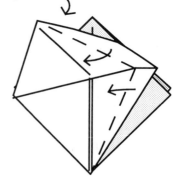

4) Pinch the two top corners and swing the bottom corners together...

5) ...like this. Flatten by swinging a flap to the left and a flap to the right.

6) Wow. Fold the lower left edge of **one flap** to the center line.

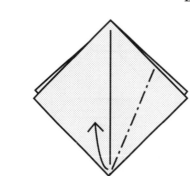

Does not lie flat!

7) Unfold step 6.

8) Using the creases just made, we're going to push the right flap inside. Raise **one layer** of paper up from the bottom...

9) ...like this. No new creases here! Fold the right edges inside along the existing creases...

Still does not lie flat!

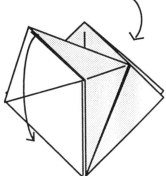

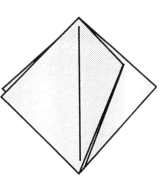

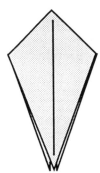

10) ...like this. Fold the layer back down.

11) Yeah! Repeat steps 6-10 on the other three flaps.

12) Done! Fold two of these to make an Ornament.

To make the Ornament

Insert one into the other, alternating which flap gets tucked inside and which goes outside. Push together as tightly as possible.

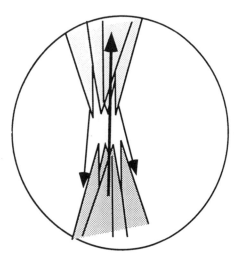

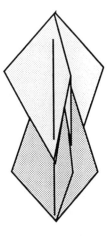

Origami earrings fit any occasion.

39

Three Wise Men

They're royal! They're dapper!
They're cubist! They're a modular fold with
numerous variations. Each wise guy requires
five squares of paper.

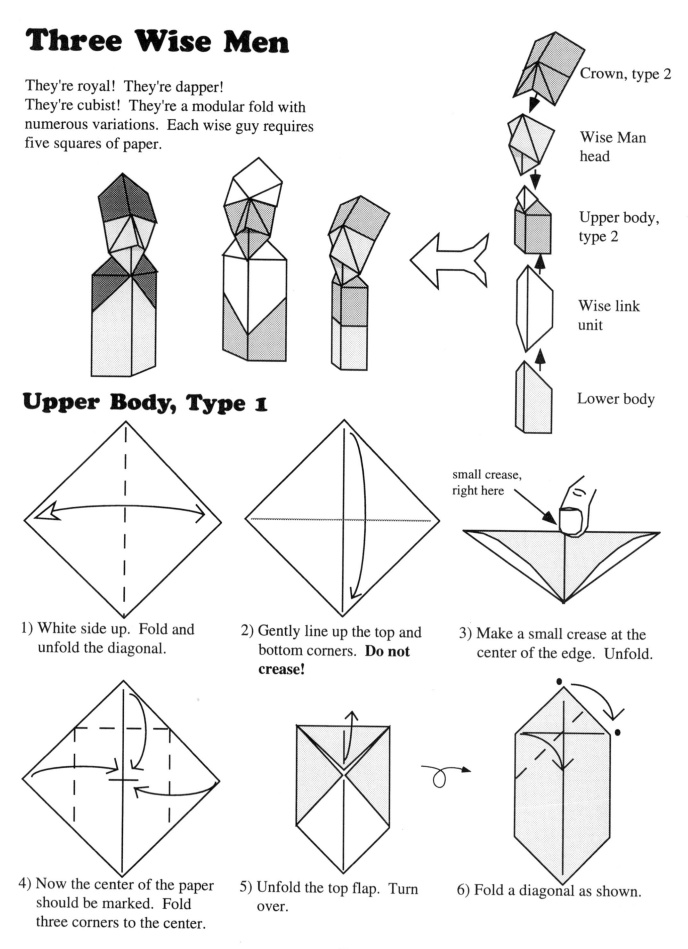

Crown, type 2

Wise Man
head

Upper body,
type 2

Wise link
unit

Lower body

Upper Body, Type 1

small crease,
right here

1) White side up. Fold and
unfold the diagonal.

2) Gently line up the top and
bottom corners. **Do not
crease!**

3) Make a small crease at the
center of the edge. Unfold.

4) Now the center of the paper
should be marked. Fold
three corners to the center.

5) Unfold the top flap. Turn
over.

6) Fold a diagonal as shown.

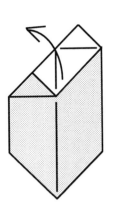

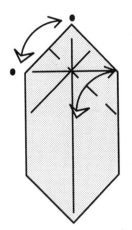

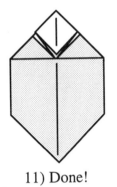

7) Unfold step 6.

8) Repeat steps 6 and 7 in the other direction.

9) Using the creases just made, bring the corners to the center...

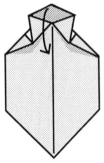

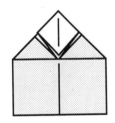

10) ...like this, bringing the top corner down too...

11) Done!

Upper Body, Type 2

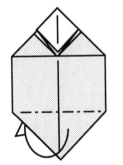

1) This is easy. Just take the type 1 body and fold the bottom corner behind to the center.

2) Done! Note the close resemblance to the Type 1 upper body.

Lower Body

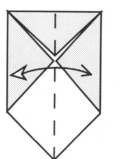

1) Follow steps 1-4 of the upper body. Fold and unfold along the middle crease.

2) Flip over and you're done! Wasn't that easy?

Body Link Unit

(This is used to link the upper and lower body parts.)

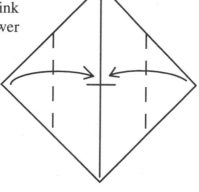

1) Follow steps 1-3 of the upper body. Fold the left and right corners to the center.

2) Wow! You're done!

Linking the Upper and Lower Bodies

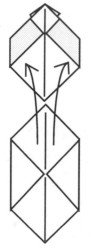

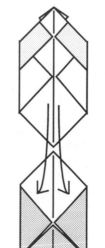

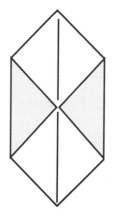

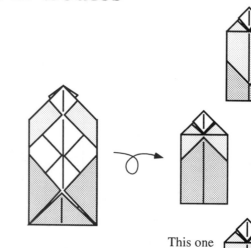

1) Insert a body link into the upper body.

2) Then fit the lower part of the link into the lower body...

3) ...like this. Obtain the variations by playing with the way in which the upper and lower bodies overlap.

This one uses the Type 2 upper body.

Wise Head

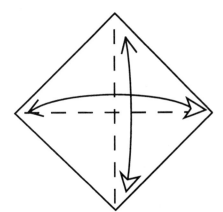

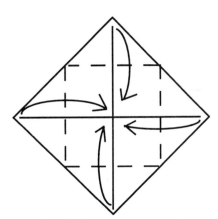

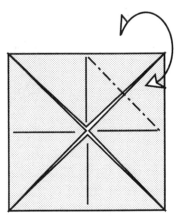

1) White side up. Fold and unfold both diagonals.

2) Fold all four corners to the center.

3) (Enlarged view) Fold one corner behind to the center and unfold.

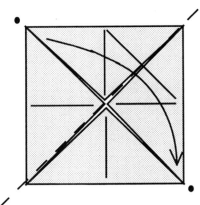

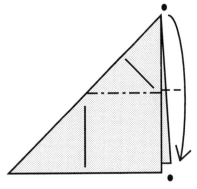

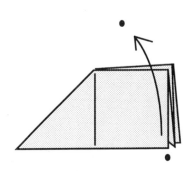

4) Fold along the diagonal, as shown.

5) Push one flap inside the model (that is, reverse-fold it)...

6) ...like this. Raise **one layer** up and peek underneath...

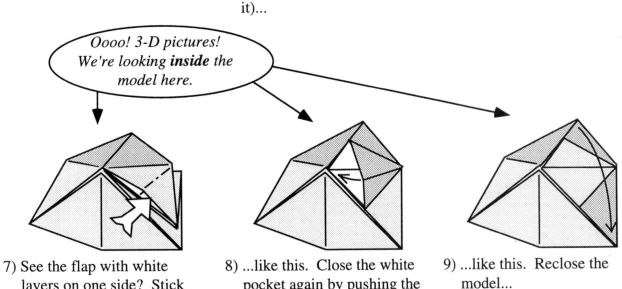

Oooo! 3-D pictures! We're looking inside the model here.

7) See the flap with white layers on one side? Stick your finger in the layers to open up the flap...

8) ...like this. Close the white pocket again by pushing the point into the center...

9) ...like this. Reclose the model...

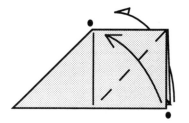

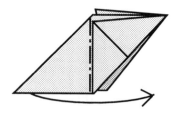

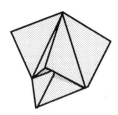

10) ...and we're flat again! Fold the bottom right corner up. **Repeat behind.**

11) Here's another reverse-fold! Reverse the left point all the way through using existing creases.

12) Now we're going to reverse-fold again, so that the point sticks out at a right angle...

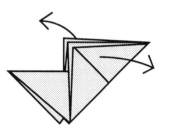

13) ...like this! Spread apart the two side flaps.

14) The completed Wise Head!

Wise Crown, Type 1

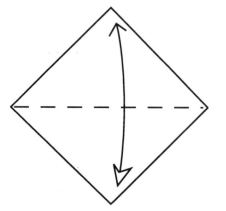

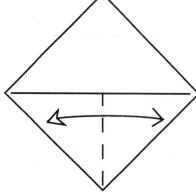

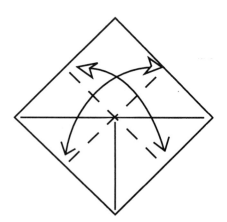

1) White side up. Fold and unfold a diagonal.

2) Fold and unfold the other diagonal too, **but only half-way!**

3) Now fold from side to side in both directions (and unfold).

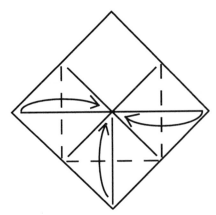

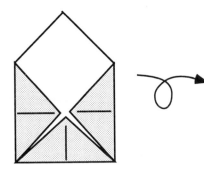

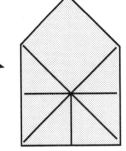

4) Fold three corners to the center.

5) Turn over.

6) Done with the first Crown!

Wise Crown, Type 2

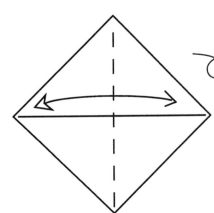

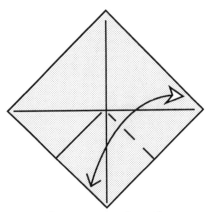

1) Begin as in the first crown, but crease both diagonals all the way. **Turn over.**

2) Now crease from side to side, **but only halfway!**

3) Do the same in the other direction.

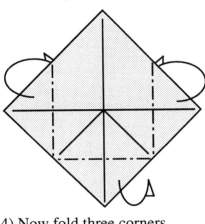

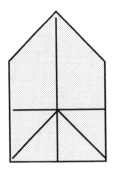

4) Now fold three corners behind to the center (as in the first Crown).

5) Done with the second Crown!

Wise Crown, Type 3

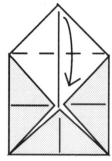 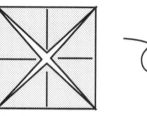 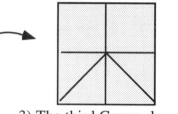

1) Begin with a turned-over second Crown. Fold the top corner to the center.

2) Turn over.

3) The third Crown done!

Crowning the Wise Head

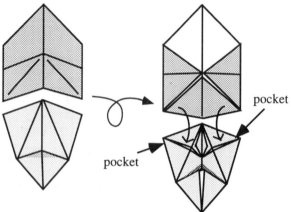 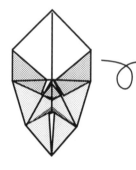 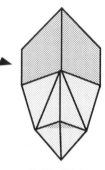

pocket

pocket

1) Take a crown and a head and turn 'em over.

2) Insert the two corners of the crown into the two pockets in back of the head...

3) ...like this.

4) Voilà!

FINALLY! Joining the Body and Head

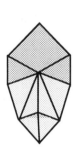 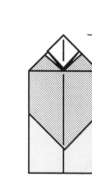 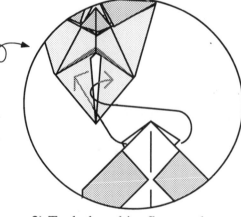 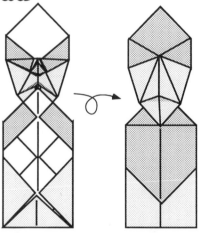

1) Get a head and a body. Turn over.

2) Tuck the white flaps at the top of the body **into** the flaps in back of the "chin."

3) After you turn your Wise Man over, you should take him to parties and introduce him to other royal dignitaries.

Sea Serpent

Four squares of paper are needed to create the illusion of a seaworthy Serpent!

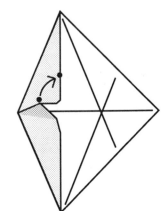

Serpent Head

1) White side up. Fold and unfold both diagonals.

2) Bring two sides to the center line...

3) ...like this. Then undo step 2.

4) Repeat steps 2-3 with the other half of the paper.

5) Now we have a bunch of creases. Fold the two on the left half at the same time...

6) ...like this. Let the short flap point up (i.e., press it flat).

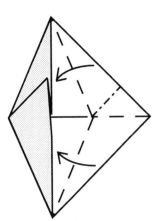

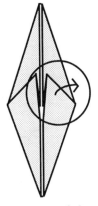

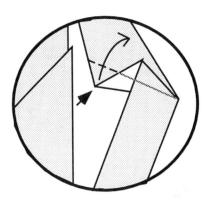

7) Repeat steps 5-6 on the right.

8) Zoom in on one of the flaps. Unfold it slightly.

9) Careful here. Push the inside paper out as shown in the next picture...

47

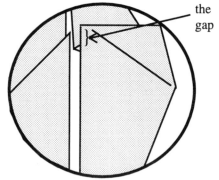

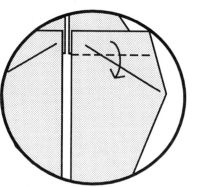

the
gap

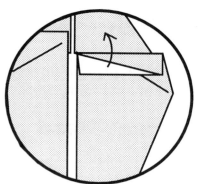

10) ...like this. Notice "the gap."
You need "the gap." **Repeat**
step 9 on the left.

11) There. Now fold the right
flap down...

12) ...like this. Undo step 11.

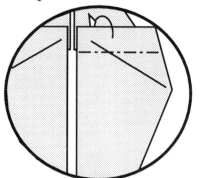

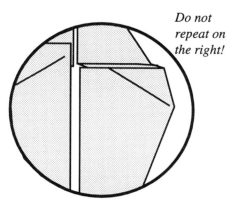

*Do not
repeat on
the right!*

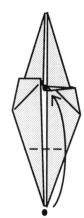

13) Using the creases just
made, make a pocket by
folding the flap inside...

14) ...like this. All right! Back
to normal view.

15) Fold the bottom point up.

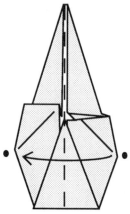

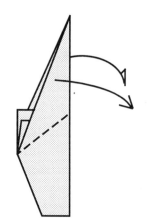

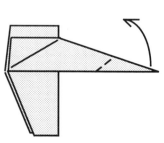

16) (Enlarged view) Fold the
whole thing in half.

17) Reverse the "snout" down...

18) ...like this. Reverse the tip
up to make a horn.

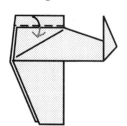

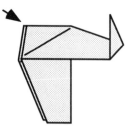

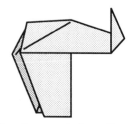

19) Tuck the top flap into the
pocket beside it.

20) Push down on the top
corner to make the head
more 3-D.

21) The Serpent's head!

48

Serpent Body

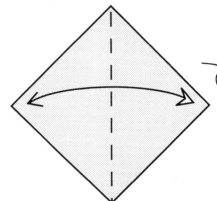

1) Colored side up. Fold and unfold the vertical diagonal. **Turn over.**

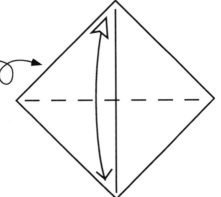

2) Fold and unfold the other diagonal.

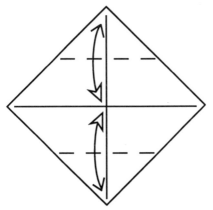

3) Fold the top and bottom corners to the center and back.

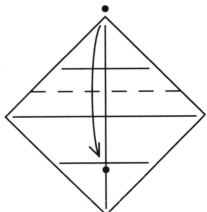

4) Fold the top corner to the indicated crease mark.

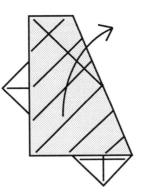

5) Unfold. **Repeat** steps 4 and 5 with the bottom corner.

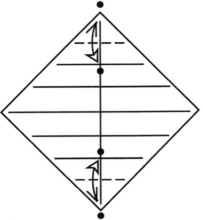

6) Fold the top and bottom corners to the indicated crease. Unfold.

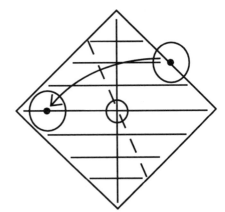

7) Watch the landmarks here. Fold a diagonal crease, going through the center, so that the midpoint of the upper right edge falls on the indicated diagonal...

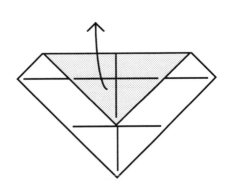

8) ...like this. Unfold step 7.

9) Now fold the two creases in the upper half to make a "crimp." **The model will not lie flat!**

49

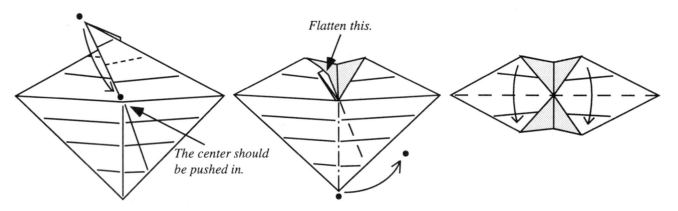

Flatten this.

The center should be pushed in.

10) The model should look concave. Bring the top point to the center along existing creases. Some of the paper should spread apart as you do this...

11) ...like this. Flatten what you just folded with a good crease. **Then repeat** steps 9-10 on the bottom point.

12) You should end up with this. Fold in half.

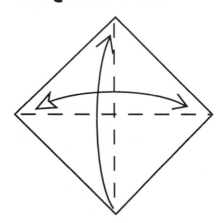

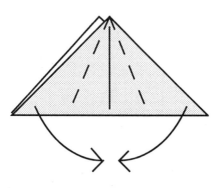

13) Round out the body by folding along the existing creases.

14) Completed body segment!

Serpent Tail

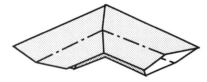

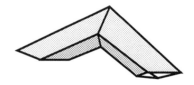

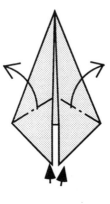

1) White side up. Fold and unfold the vertical diagonal. **Then** fold the other diagonal (and leave it folded).

2) Fold the "legs" of the triangle to the center line.

3) Unfold a **single layer** on the left and right, spreading the corners as you do so...

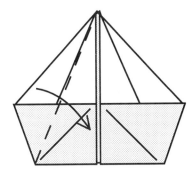

4) ...like this. Fold the upper left edge to the center line.

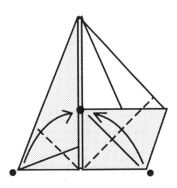

5) Now fold the two bottom corners to the center.

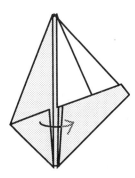

6) Insert the left flap into the right pocket. **The model will become 3-D and stay that way!**

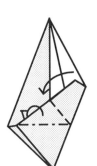

7) Close up the tail by folding the right flap down inside.

8) Whoa! Turn over.

9) The tail is all done!

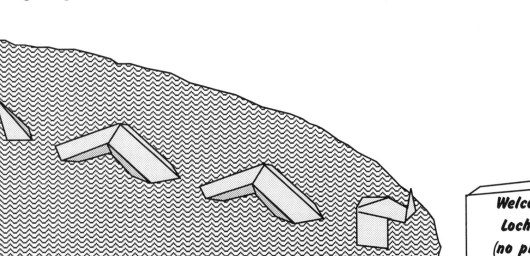

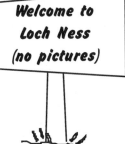

Welcome to
Loch Ness
(no pictures)

51

Sunburst

This model utilizes two types of units and needs 16 squares of paper to complete!

The First Unit

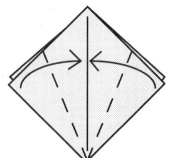

1) Follow steps 1-6 of the Ornamental Thingie (page 38). Fold the lower edge of the left and right flaps to the center line.

2) Fold the top point down as shown.

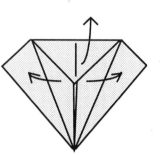

3) Undo steps 1 and 2.

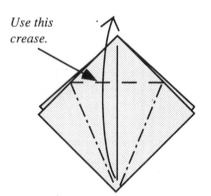

Use this crease.

4) Lift **one layer** of paper up. Use the crease from step 2!

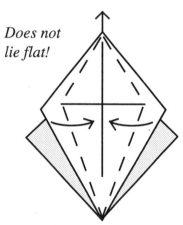

Does not lie flat!

5) Fold the flap all the way up. Let the sides come together...

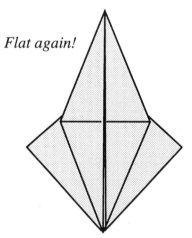

Flat again!

6) ...like this. **Repeat** steps 1-5 behind.

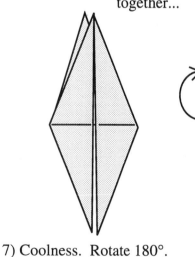

7) Coolness. Rotate 180°.

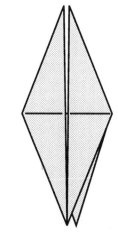

8) Done with the first type of unit. Fold 8 of these.

The Second Unit

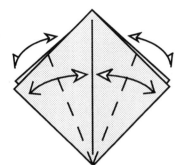 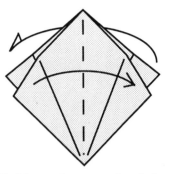 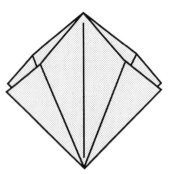

1) Begin as in the 1st unit, but this time fold and unfold to the center line, and also **repeat behind!**

2) Fold one layer to the right, and one to the left in back.

3) Done with the 2nd unit! Fold 8 of these.

To assemble the Sunburst

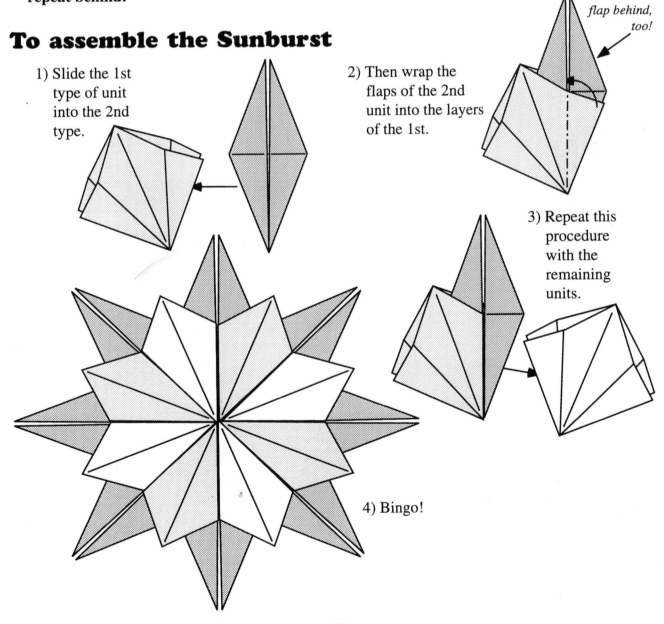

1) Slide the 1st type of unit into the 2nd type.

2) Then wrap the flaps of the 2nd unit into the layers of the 1st.

Tuck in the flap behind, too!

3) Repeat this procedure with the remaining units.

4) Bingo!

53

Stabile

This model is irregularly regular, which is a clever way to say that it's hard to visualize until you have one in front of you. It may stand or be hung, and generally fits into the "Christmas tree ornament" class of objects.

The name refers to the sculptor Alexander Calder's collection of models that stand on the ground (as opposed to his mobiles).

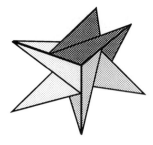

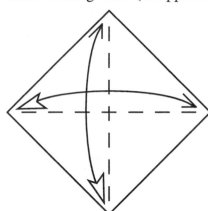

1) White side up. Fold and unfold both diagonals.

2) Bring two sides to the center line...

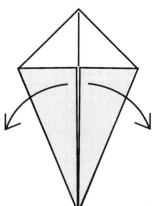

3) ...like this. Then undo step 2.

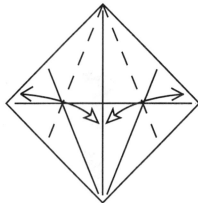

4) Repeat steps 2-3 with the other half of the paper.

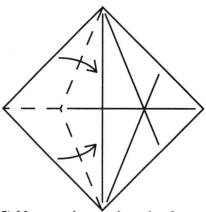

5) Now we have a bunch of creases. Fold the two on the left half at the same time...

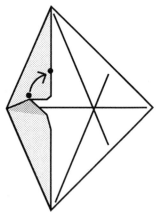

6) ...like this. Let the short flap point up (i.e., press it flat).

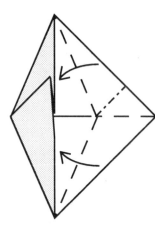

7) Repeat steps 5-6 on the right.

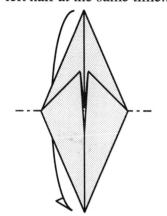

8) Fold the top down behind.

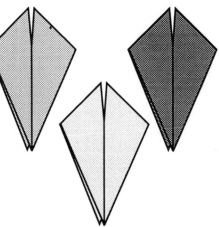

9) Done! Make 3 of 'em!

To assemble the Stabile

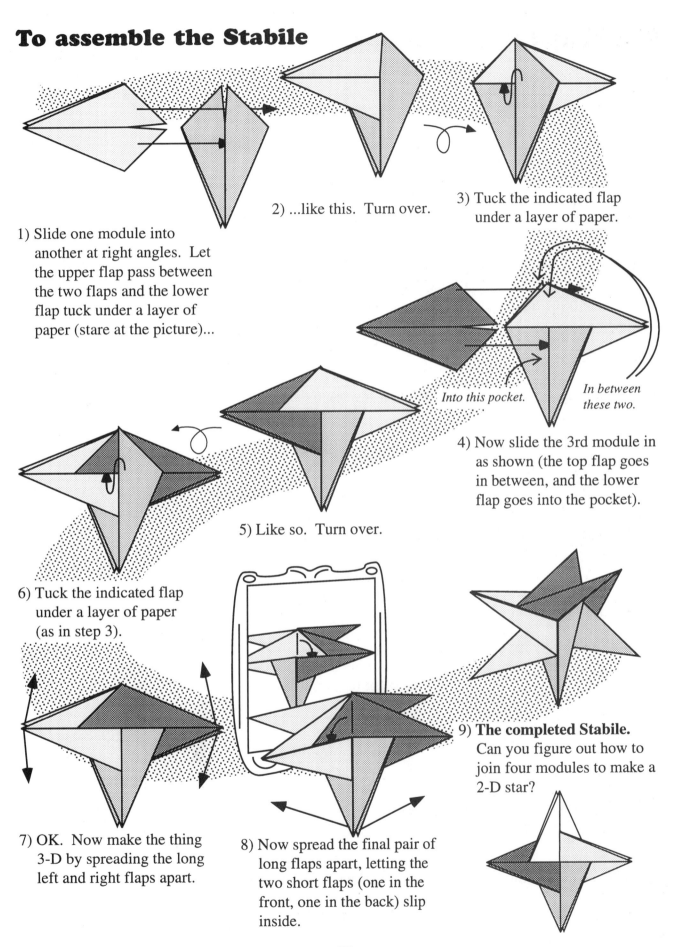

1) Slide one module into another at right angles. Let the upper flap pass between the two flaps and the lower flap tuck under a layer of paper (stare at the picture)...

2) ...like this. Turn over.

3) Tuck the indicated flap under a layer of paper.

Into this pocket.

In between these two.

4) Now slide the 3rd module in as shown (the top flap goes in between, and the lower flap goes into the pocket).

5) Like so. Turn over.

6) Tuck the indicated flap under a layer of paper (as in step 3).

7) OK. Now make the thing 3-D by spreading the long left and right flaps apart.

8) Now spread the final pair of long flaps apart, letting the two short flaps (one in the front, one in the back) slip inside.

9) **The completed Stabile.** Can you figure out how to join four modules to make a 2-D star?

55

The Squared Square

Squares (and thus cubes) hold a special place in origami. This fold finds squares in an unusual way.

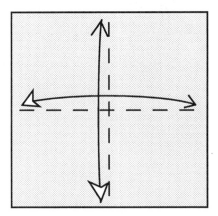

1) Colored side up. Fold and unfold.

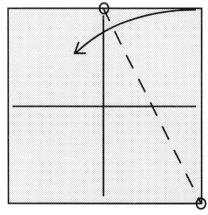

2) Fold the upper right corner to the left, using the circled corners as guides.

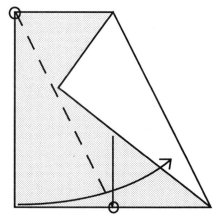

3) Repeat with the lower left corner.

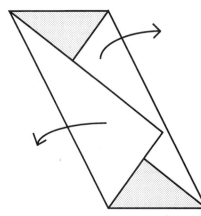

4) Unfold steps 2 and 3.

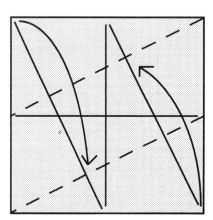

5) Repeat steps 2 and 3 on the other two corners. Make sure you get the orientation right!

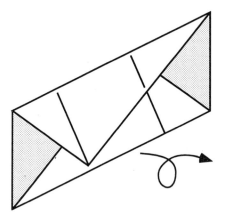

6) Turn over.

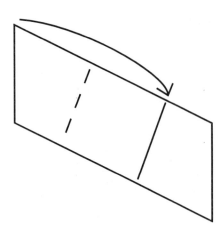

7) Fold along the existing crease.

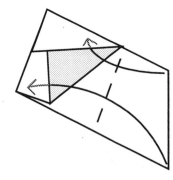

8) Fold the other end in the same way, tucking it into the first flap.

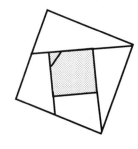

9) The Squared Square!

56

To make the Squared Square Cube

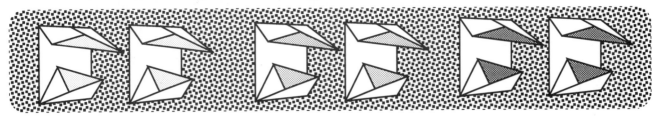

1) Make three pairs of Squared Squares, each pair a different color. Unfold step 8.

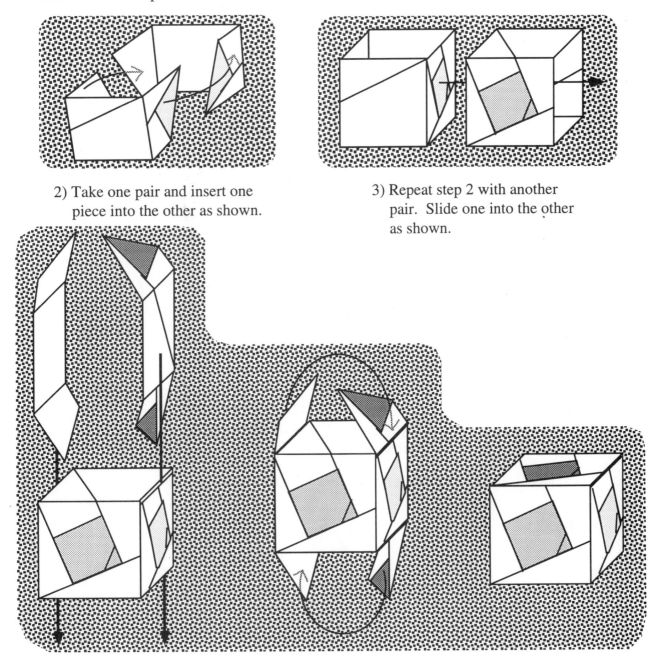

2) Take one pair and insert one piece into the other as shown.

3) Repeat step 2 with another pair. Slide one into the other as shown.

4) Slide the last two pieces into the slots made by the first two pairs.

5) Lock the loose ends together as in step 8 of the Squared Square.

6) The finished Squared Square Cube!

Chess Set

Folding an origami chess set takes a lot of time and a lot of paper. Yet working through this whole set is excellent practice for learning basic folding techniques.

The Pawn (Begin with one half of the Ornamental Thingie, page 38.)

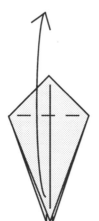

1) Fold **one** flap up.

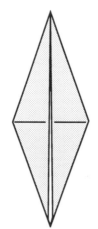

2) Turn over.

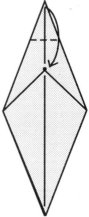

3) Fold the top point to the blunt point.

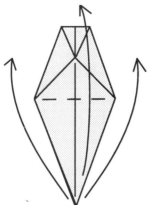

4) Repeat steps 1-3 on the other 3 flaps.

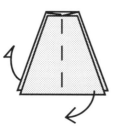

5) Separate the layers to make it stand.

6) The Pawn! You will need 8 for each side.

The Stand (Each of the remaining pieces requires one.)

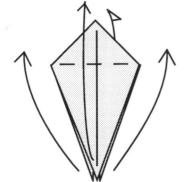

1) Start as for the Pawn, but fold all four flaps up.

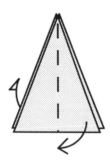

2) Make it 3-D.

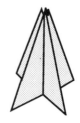

3) The standing stand! You will need one for each non-pawn piece (8 per side).

58

The Rook

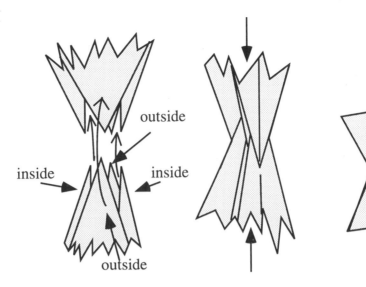

1) The Rook is made with two stands. Position the stands as shown above.

2) Here's a confusing picture. Slide the two stands into each other by overlapping the flaps symmetrically.

3) Push them all the way together, and you're all done with the Rook!

The Knight

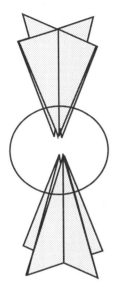

1) Take a stand (ha!) and turn it upside down. Fold the top two corners to the center line.

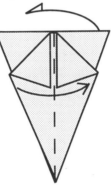

2) Fold one flap to the right in the front and one to the left in the back.

3) Swivel the left flap up...

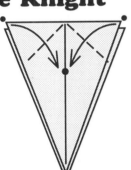

Press here.

4) ...like this. Squeeze the top to make the flap stay put.

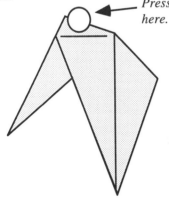

5) Give the horsey a schnoz by folding the tip inside.

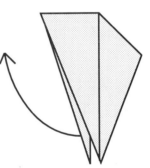

Wuff

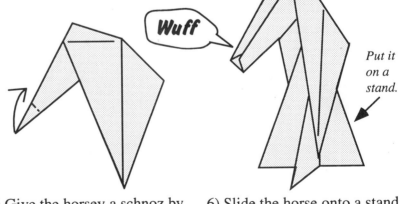

Put it on a stand.

6) Slide the horse onto a stand as for the Rook, and the Knight has just begun!

The Bishop (Begin with step 6 of the Ornamental Thingie, page 38.)

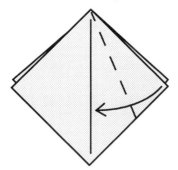

1) Fold the top edge of a flap to the center line.

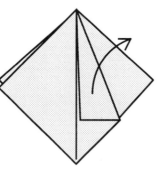

2) Unfold the flap.

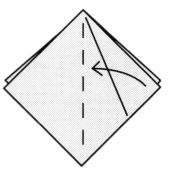

3) Raise the right flap up...

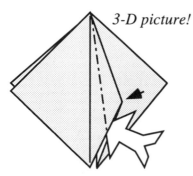

3-D picture!

4) ...and squash it flat (look at the next picture).

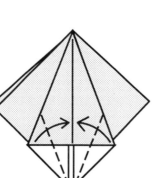

5) This is what the squash should look like. Fold the sides to the center.

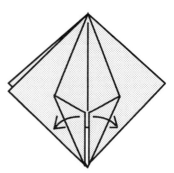

6) Unfold step 5.

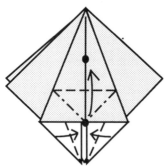

7) Now using the creases just made, lift the center of the horizontal edge up...

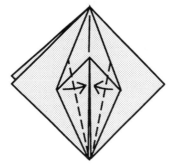

8) ...like this. Fold the sides to the center.

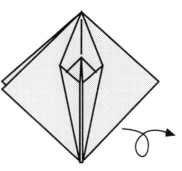

9) Turn over.

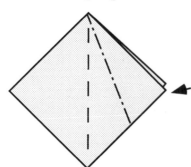

10) Repeat steps 1-8 on the right.

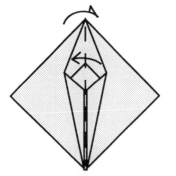

11) Fold the skinny flap to the left. Repeat behind.

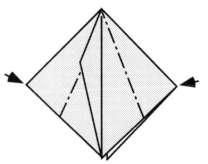

12) Repeat steps 1-8 on the right. Repeat behind!

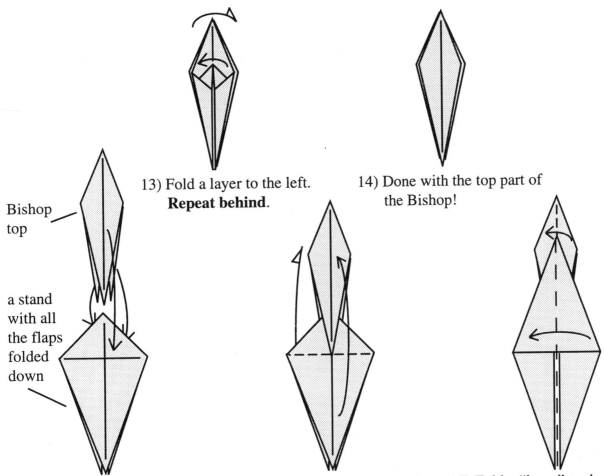

13) Fold a layer to the left. **Repeat behind**.

14) Done with the top part of the Bishop!

Bishop top

a stand with all the flaps folded down

15) Now make a stand and fold all four flaps down (so it looks like part of an Ornamental Thingie). Slide the Bishop top around the blunt point so that the two side flaps go into pockets. Push together only as far as the next picture shows.

16) Fold one flap of the stand over the Bishop top. **Repeat behind**.

17) Fold a "layer" to the left. **Repeat behind**.

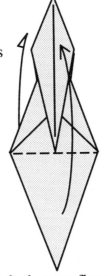

18) Fold the bottom flap over the Bishop top. Repeat behind, spread the layers to make it stand, and you're done!

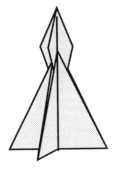

19) Look! It's the Bishop!

The King

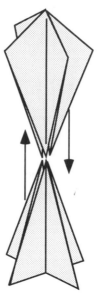

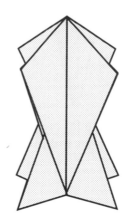

1)Take one half of an Ornamental Thingie (page 38)
and slide it into a stand as
done for the rook.

2) Push together all the way
and you're done!

The Queen

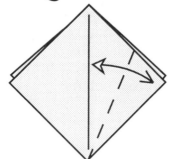

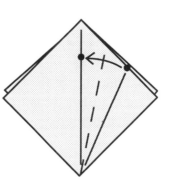

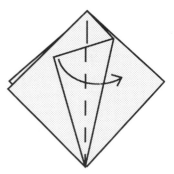

1) Start with step 6 of the
Ornamental Thingie (page
38). Fold the lower edge of a
flap to the center line. Unfold.

2) Then fold the flap to the left
again so that the crease from
step 1 lands on the center
line.

3) Fold the flap to the right
along the center line.

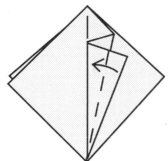

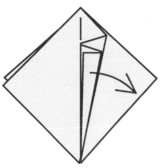

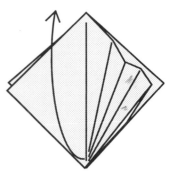

4) Fold the flap back to the
center line.

5) You should see this cool
zigzag pattern. Unfold steps
2-4.

6) Now lift a **single layer** up.
We'll get 3-D for a few steps
here.

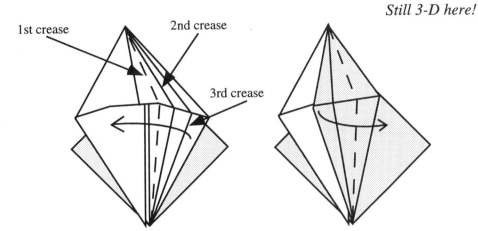

Still 3-D here!

1st crease 2nd crease

3rd crease

7) Look at the creases inside. Fold the right edge to the left along the "1st crease."

8) Now fold to the right along the "2nd crease."

9) Finally, do the "3rd crease."

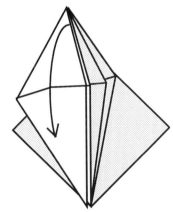

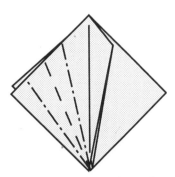

Flat again!

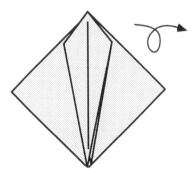

10) Close the flap back up.

11) Repeat steps 1-10 on the right.

12) Turn over! (You can guess what's coming.)

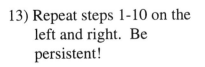

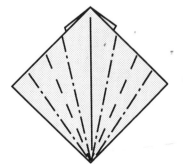

13) Repeat steps 1-10 on the left and right. Be persistent!

14) Fold the top point down.

15) **Crease firmly**. Unfold step 14.

63

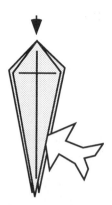
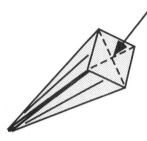

16) Flatten the top point to make a square. You'll need to get your fingers inside the Queen to do this. Don't be shy.

17) Push the center of the square in. Flatten the Queen up again by folding the diagonals.

18) Done with the top part of the queen!

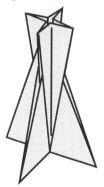

19) Slide the Queen top into a stand (as done for the Rook, Knight, and King).

Note: Origami chess is best played indoors. Avoid strong winds.

A Frog's Tale

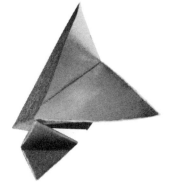

There once was a frog named
Bigmouth who was bored with life.

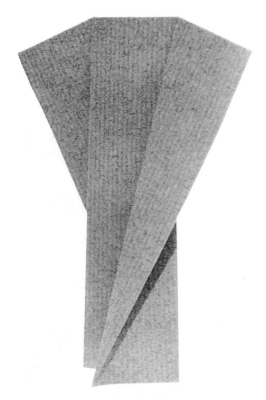

He had long hid from owl...

swum with fish...

dodged the feet of ambitious elephants...

and croaked back at scottie dog. But Bigmouth was hungry for new experience.

Bigmouth went in search of action. He was talked to by bird...

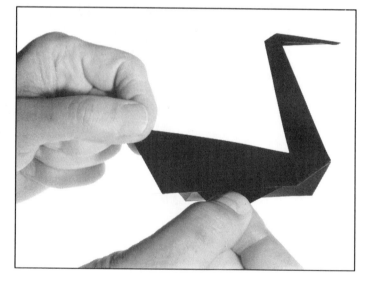

pecked at by funky swan...

and almost poisoned by cobra.

A somersaulting frog won from him a princess...

who had kissed him with a mouth as big as his own!

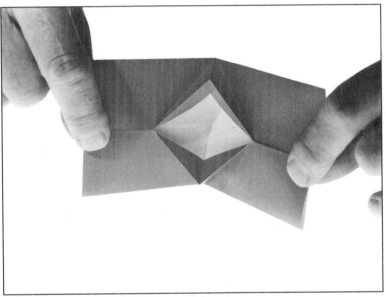

Stopped by love's dart, Bigmouth hibernated.

Bigmouth awoke in a strange land where he encountered a wheel that changed shape...

and things worn in the ears...

of three wise men.

Bigmouth crossed an inland sea on the back of a serpent...

riding the waves under a many-colored sun.   On the far shore he contemplated a starlike shape...

a squared square and an askew cube.

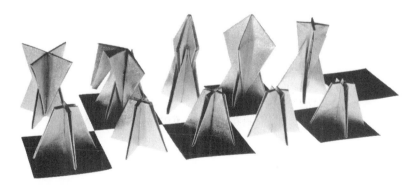

Farther inland, Bigmouth came upon figures that battled on a checkered board.
Although intrigued by the game, he became lonely for his own kind.

Bigmouth was then transported to the Great Pond for All Good Frogs. Plopping and splashing, he played with his brothers and sisters. But since it was not yet time for him, they sent him back to find his way home.

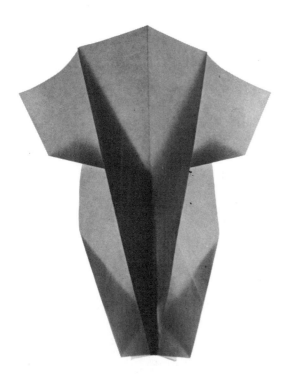

swam with some angelfish...

Bigmouth continued on his journey. He
carefully avoided an imposing elephant...

listened to nature with a friendly dog...

and hopscotched with a rabbit.

Bigmouth then hitched a ride with an eagle...

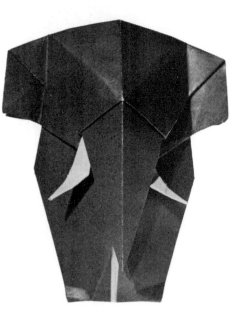

who dumped him into a school of hungry fish!

An enormous elephant saved Bigmouth
from being eaten alive and carried him
home in the left nostril of his trunk.

Bigmouth was finally content to do just what he did best,
by virtue of his big mouth: eat and talk with friends.

Frog Pond

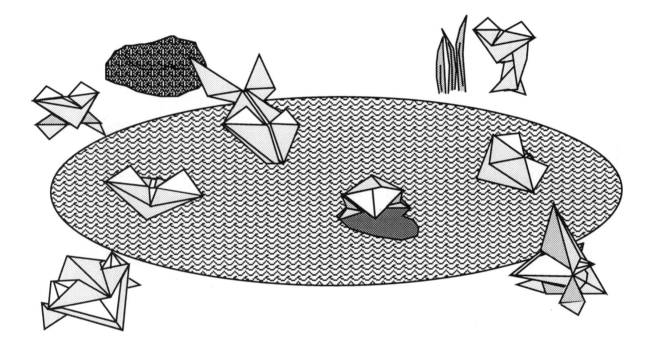

Frog Head with a Big Mouth

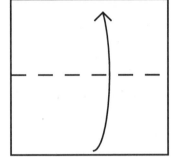

1) Start with the white side up. Fold the bottom edge to the top.

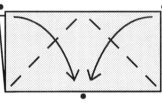

2) Fold the top corners to the bottom center, **one layer only!**

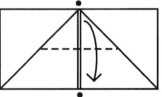

3) Fold the top point of the triangle to the bottom center.

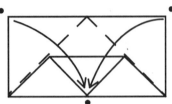

4) Again, fold the top two corners to the bottom center.

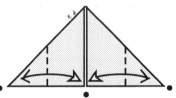

5) Fold and unfold the bottom two corners to the center.

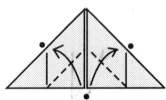

6) Fold the flaps at the bottom center to the diagonal edge.

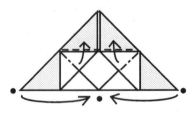

7) Form eyes by swiveling the white triangles up while spreading open the two corners...

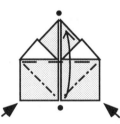

8) ...like this. Now fold the **hidden white flap** at the bottom to the top, while spreading the bottom corners open...

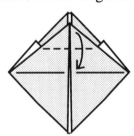

9) ...like this. Fold the top point down to the center.

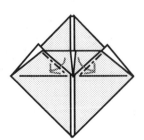

10) Lock the flap in this position by folding the layers underneath it into the model.

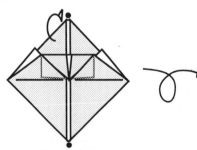

11) Notice the X-ray view. Swing the far half to the bottom, and turn over.

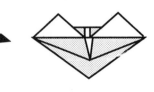

12) The Frog Head done!

Frog with a Big Mouth in Flight!

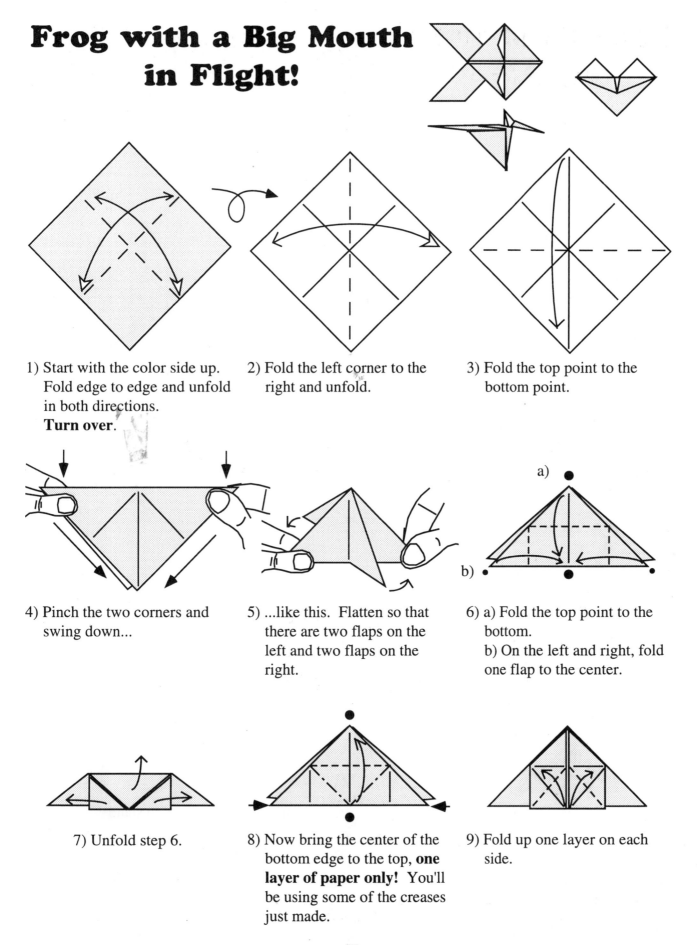

1) Start with the color side up. Fold edge to edge and unfold in both directions. **Turn over**.

2) Fold the left corner to the right and unfold.

3) Fold the top point to the bottom point.

4) Pinch the two corners and swing down...

5) ...like this. Flatten so that there are two flaps on the left and two flaps on the right.

6) a) Fold the top point to the bottom.
   b) On the left and right, fold one flap to the center.

7) Unfold step 6.

8) Now bring the center of the bottom edge to the top, **one layer of paper only!** You'll be using some of the creases just made.

9) Fold up one layer on each side.

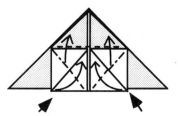

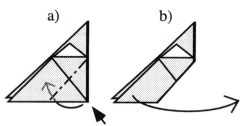

10) Form the eyes by swinging the triangles up...

11) ...like this. Fold in half away from you.

12) a) Reverse the corner inside the model...
   b) ...to look like this. Then open up by bringing a layer to the right.

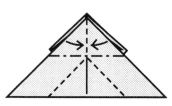

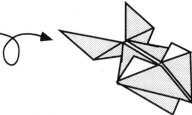

13) Make sure the model is flat. Then make it 3-D by raising the lower "jaw" and using the existing creases...

Does not lie flat! →

14) ...like this. Turn over and...

15) ...you're done!

Try your hand at making these variations from the finished Frog in Flight!

Lotus Position

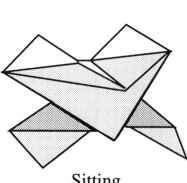

Sitting

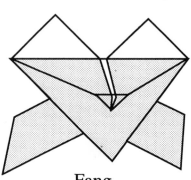

Fang

"Fang" may be used to stand the frog on its nose, as if it were diving into water!

Frog with a Big Mouth, Tongue, and Eyes

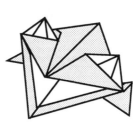

This is definitely the most detailed and challenging frog in this series of amphibians.

1) OK. White side up. Fold and unfold both diagonals.

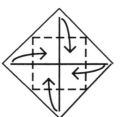

2) Fold all four corners to the center.

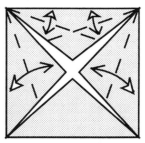

3) (Enlarged view) Make four creases on the flaps as shown. Try to be accurate!

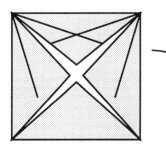

4) Turn over.

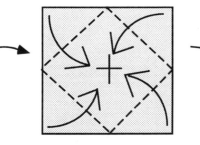

5) Fold the corners to the center again and **turn over**.

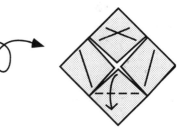

6) Fold the bottom flap **almost** to the corner. (This'll be the tongue!)

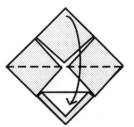

7) Fold along the diagonal.

8) Fold the top flaps to the side of the triangle.

9) Return the flaps to their former position and zoom in on the left side.

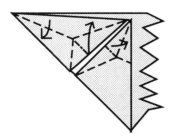

10) Refold step 8, but this time spread the edges of the paper to the side as shown.

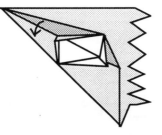

11) Step 10 in progress...

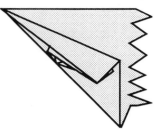

12) ...like this! Repeat step 10 on the right.

69

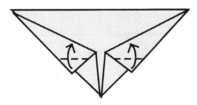

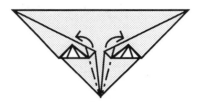

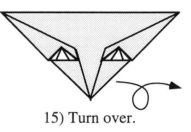

13) Fold the eyes up.

14) Fold into the model the extra paper between the eyes.

15) Turn over.

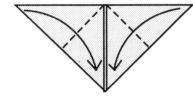

16) Fold the two side flaps to the bottom.

17) Then fold these flaps to the top.

18) Fold the two flaps to the sides.

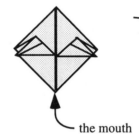

the mouth

19) Done! Turn over and open the mouth.

20) The finished Frog.

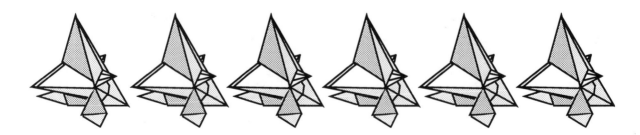

Getting Tricky

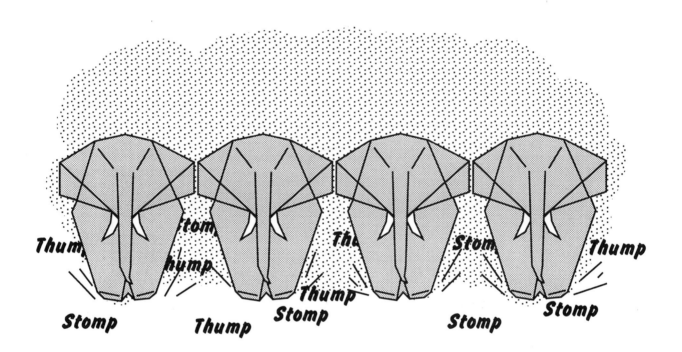

The folds in this section are, yes, a bit trickier than those in the rest of the book.
But don't be scared away! They're all written for the beginner, but
you should keep in mind that two or three attempts may be needed.

Elephant Minor

This is another quite simple fold that captures the essence of its subject.

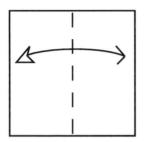

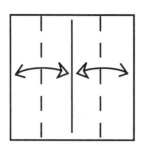

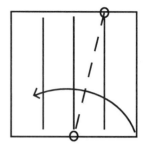

1) White side up. Fold and unfold.

2) Fold and unfold the two edges to the center crease.

3) Use the corners of one of the rectangles to make this fold.

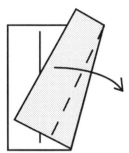

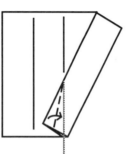

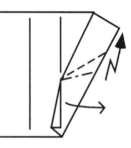

4) Fold along an existing crease.

5) Now fold the folded edge to the center line (it'll get skinny).

6) Pull out the **top layer** from under the previous fold and flatten the model with a "crimp."

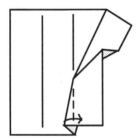

7) Fold along the existing crease.

8) Repeat steps 3-7 on the left.

9) a) Fold the little triangle up.
   b) Fold the corners up to taste.

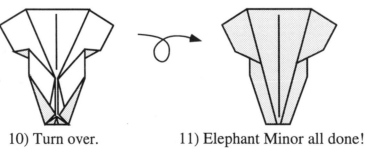

10) Turn over.

11) Elephant Minor all done! Pull out the inner flaps from step 9a to make it stand.

72

Angel Fish

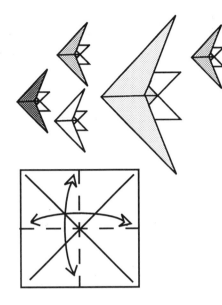

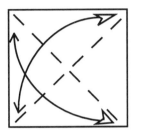

1) Start with white side up to make a fish with white tails. Fold and unfold both diagonals.

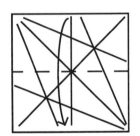

2) Fold and unfold from side to side in both directions.

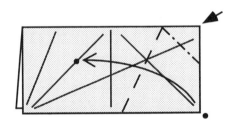

3) Fold the sides to the diagonal line and unfold.

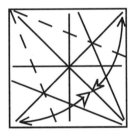

4) Repeat step 3 in the other direction.

5) Look at all the creases! Fold the top edge to the bottom.

6) Lift **one layer** of the lower right corner and swing it up along an existing crease...

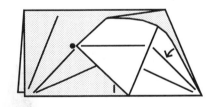

7) ... like this; we are in progress here. Flatten the model...

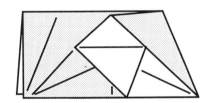

8) ...like this. **Repeat** step 6 behind.

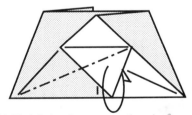

9) Fold the bottom edge into the model along an existing crease. **Repeat behind**.

73

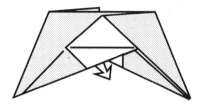

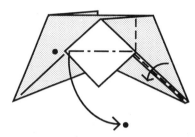

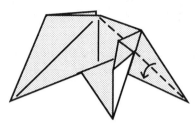

10) Pull out enough paper to make the white region a square. **Repeat behind**.

11) Swivel the corner of the white square down while folding the right flap in half.

12) Step 11 in progress...

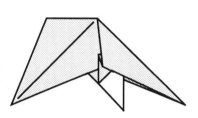

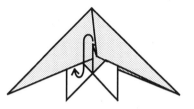

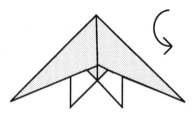

13) ...like this. **Repeat** step 11 behind.

14) Now lock the layers together by tucking the crimped flap underneath.

15) **Repeat step 14 behind**. Rotate!

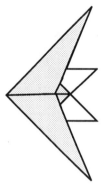

16) The Angel Fish done!

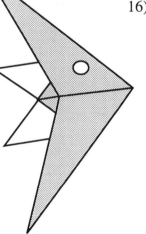

Try playing with the tail fins to create more exotic angels!

His Lady's Voice

Yes, it's a doggie. Can you figure out what
the name means?

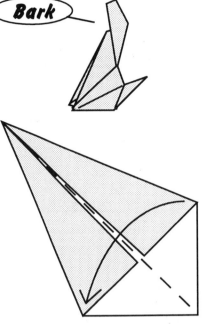

Bark

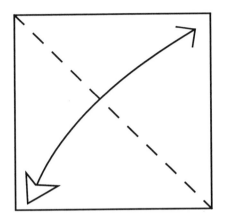

1) White side up. Fold and
unfold one diagonal.

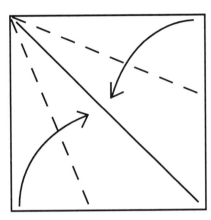

2) Fold the top and left edges to
the diagonal.

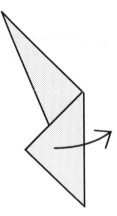

3) Fold along the diagonal.

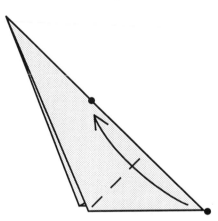

4) Fold the lower right corner
up as shown.

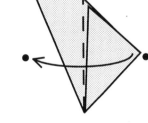

5) Fold along the line made by
the flap's edge.

6) Unfold steps 4 and 5.

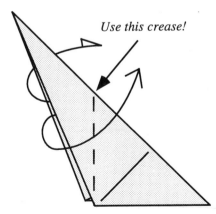

Use this crease!

7) Open the bottom a little and
"reverse" the left point. **Use
the indicated crease!**

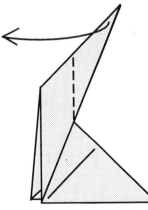

8) Fold the top point to the
left...

9) ...like so. This will be the
position of the head. Unfold
step 8.

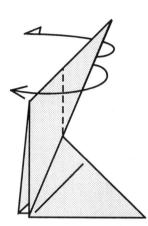 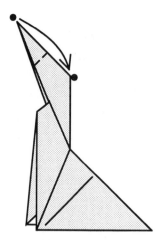 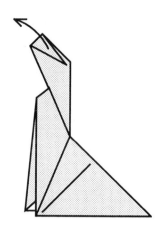

10) Use this new crease to "reverse" the point back to the left. This is similar to step 7.

11) Fold the top point to the corner.

12) Unfold step 11.

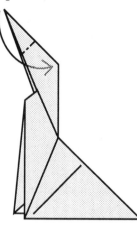 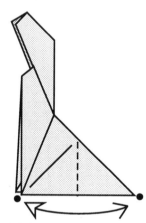 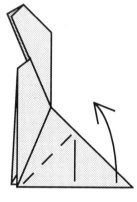

13) Now use the crease from step 11 to reverse the point **inside** the head.

14) Fold the right corner to the left. Unfold.

15) Lift the tail up a little...

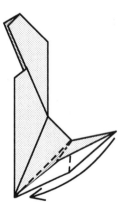 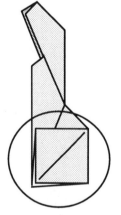 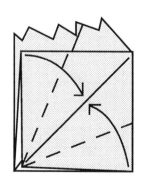

16) ...and "squash" it down as shown in the next...

17) ...picture. Zoom in on the square.

18) Fold the lower and left edges to the diagonal.

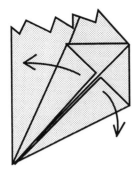 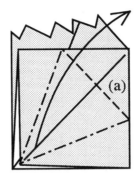 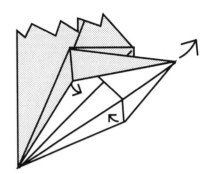

19) Unfold step 17.

20) Raise the lower left corner, **one layer only!** The crease marked (a) is not already there. **You** have to make it.

21) Step 19 in progress. Allow the sides to come together...

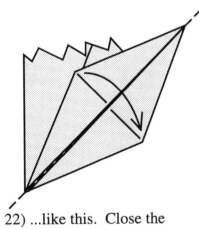 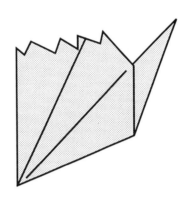 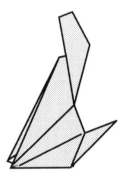

22) ...like this. Close the diamond up.

23) Back to normal view!

24) Finished dog-in-waiting, i.e., His Lady's (instead of master's, get it? Ha!) Voice.

Da Wabbit Wewised

This is a more complicated variation of the traditional Chinese rabbit.

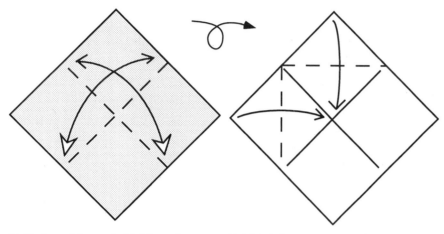

1) Color side up! Fold and unfold from side to side. Turn over.

2) Fold the top and left corners to the center.

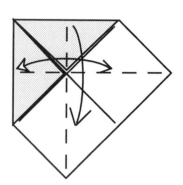

3) Fold and unfold one diagonal, then fold the other one (don't unfold).

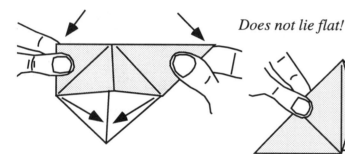

Does not lie flat!

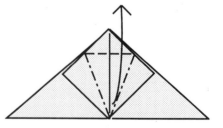

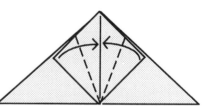

4) Pinch the two top corners and swing the two bottom corners together...

5) ...like this. Flatten symmetrically.

6) Fold the two flaps to the center line.

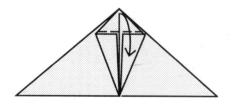

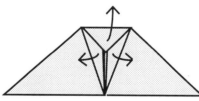

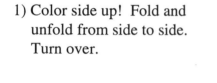

7) Fold the top point down.

8) Unfold steps 6 and 7.

9) Using the crease from step 7, raise the flap up (this is just like step 9 of the Dart, or step 20 of His Lady's Voice).

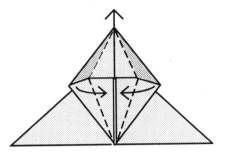

10) Pull the flap all the way up and bring the sides together.

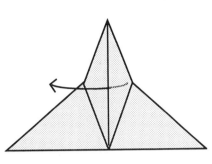

11) Pull out some paper from the right side. You will have to **open the model** a little (or a lot) to do this.

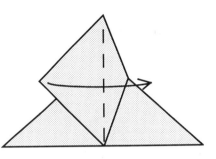

12) Fold to the right.

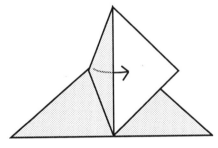

13) Repeat steps 11 and 12 on the left.

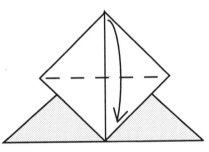

14) Fold the top point down.

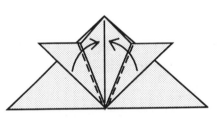

15) Fold to the center line.

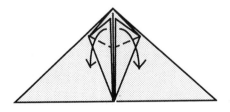

16) Fold the two flaps so that their sides point straight down.

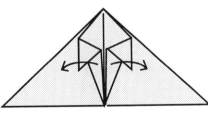

17) Open the flaps to the left and right.

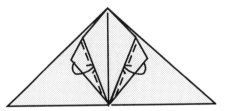

18) Now tuck each flap into the adjoining pocket...

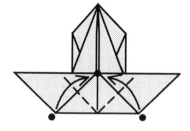 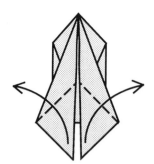 

19) ... like this. Turn over.

20) Fold the "legs" of the triangle to the center line.

21) Fold the two points up at 45° angles.

22) Fold the lower corners to the center line.

23) Fold one layer to the left and repeat behind.

24) Hold the rabbit loosely and blow into the rabbit's mouth (as if you were whistling). The result should be puffy.

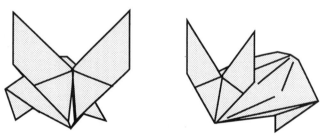

25) The finished Wabbit.

Bald Eagle

This fold, although long, is actually quite simple. It introduces a number of techniques that are used in more challenging origami, and serves as a good bridge between the simple and more complicated folds of this book.

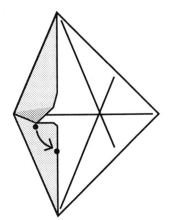

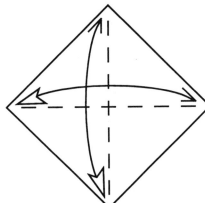

1) White side up. Crease both diagonals.

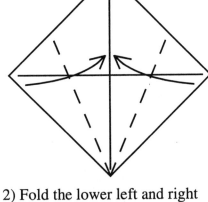

2) Fold the lower left and right edges to the center line.

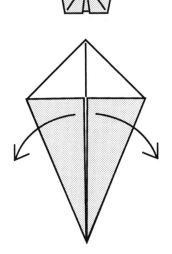

3) Unfold step 2.

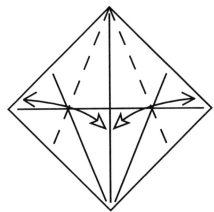

4) Now fold and unfold the **upper** left and right edges to the center line.

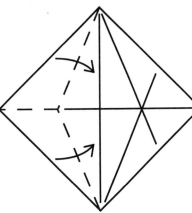

5) Now fold the two creases on the left half at the same time.

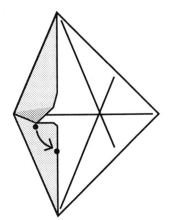

6) Like this. Let the short flap point down (i.e., press it flat).

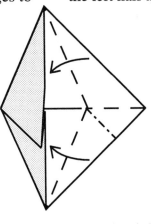

7) Repeat steps 5-6 on the right.

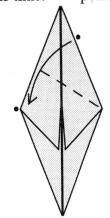

8) Fold the upper right edge down so that it lies on the leftmost corner.

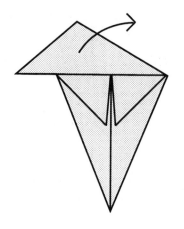

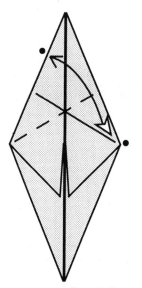

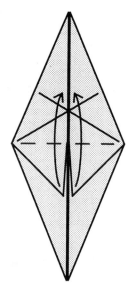

9) (Enlarged view) Unfold step 8.

10) Repeat steps 8 and 9 on the left.

11) Fold the two short flaps up.

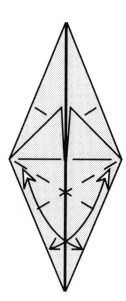

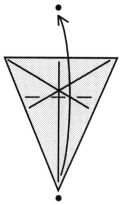

12) Repeat steps 8-10 on the lower flap.

13) Fold in half from top to bottom.

14) Then fold one layer back up, making the crease just below the intersecting creases.

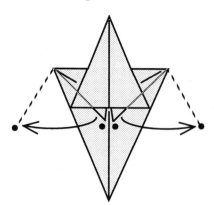

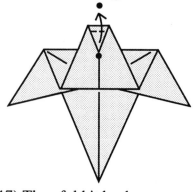

15) See the two small flaps peeking out from beneath? Pull them both to the sides...

16) ...like this, and flatten. Fold the top point down.

17) Then fold it back up, making a pleat.

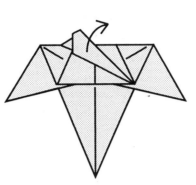

18) Right. Now fold the "beak" down to the left so it lies on the folded edge.

19) Unfold step 18.

20) Repeat step 18 in the other direction.

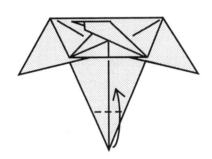

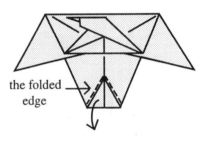

21) Now **pinch** the tip of the beak together and swing it to the left, using the creases from steps 18-20...

22) ...like this. Fold the bottom point up about 1/3 of the distance to the "breast-bone."

the folded edge

23) Now **crease** the **body** along the folded edge. Then unfold step 22.

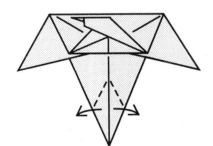

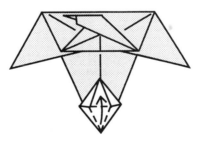

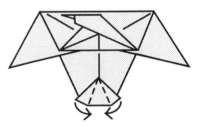

24) Using the creases from step 23, open up the bottom point...

25) ...and bring the corner up...

26) ...like this. Fold the two flaps to the center line.

83

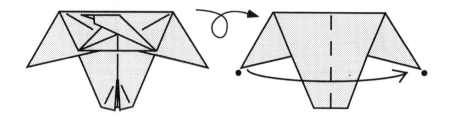

27) Here's an easy step: **turn over!**

28) Fold the whole model in half.

29) Unfold step 28.

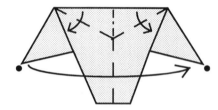

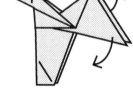

30) Now refold step 28, but this time swing the top edge inside to create "shoulders."

31) Neat, eh? Curl the beak to make it look eagle-ish.

32) Spread your wings! Adjust the feet to make the eagle stand.

Coo!

33) The finished Bald Eagle!

Tessellating Fish

This origami fish tessellates—that is, if you made enough you could tile your bathroom floor with them!

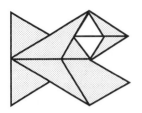

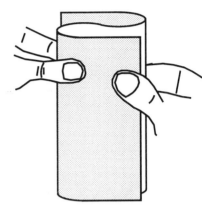

1) First you need to fold a large square into **thirds** lengthwise. Roll the square as shown and "guesstimate" where the 1/3 lines are.

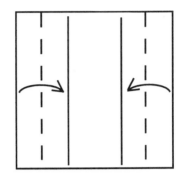

2) Once the 1/3 lines are creased, look at the paper white side up. Fold the left and right edges to the 1/3 lines.

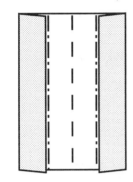

3) Then fold the center line and the 1/3 creases again to make a pleated strip.

4) Fold **one layer** of paper up, but *don't crease all the way!*

5) Unfold step 4.

6) Now, using all layers, fold the lower left corner to the crease line (see the next picture).

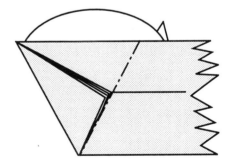

7) Then fold the corner behind.

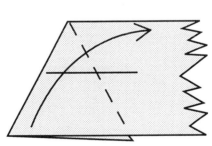

8) Then fold the corner up to the edge.

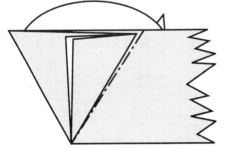

9) And so on.... Keep repeating steps 7 and 8 until all of the strip is used.

85

10) Wow! Now **unfold completely!**

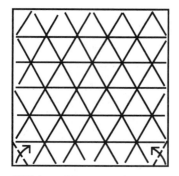

11) **White side up.** We won't be making any new creases for a while now. Position the paper like this and fold the two corners in.

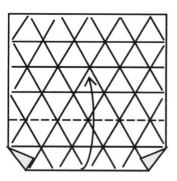

12) Fold up along the 2nd crease from the bottom edge.

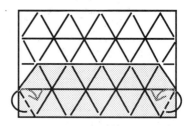

13) Reverse the two lower corners **inside**.

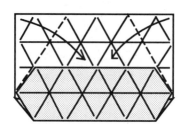

14) Fold the two upper corners as shown.

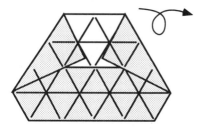

15) Great! Now turn over.

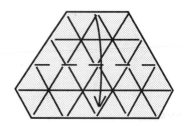

16) Fold da top to da bottom.

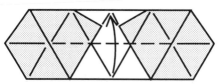

17) (Enlarged view) Fold **one layer** to the top again.

This will become 3-D!

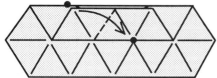

18) Holding the model loosely, bring the indicated corner down and right.

3-D picture!

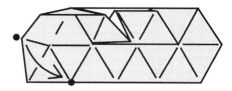

19) Then let the left side follow to the right as well...

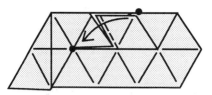

20) ...like this. Repeat steps 17-19 on the right.

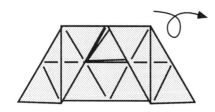

21) The model should now look like this. Turn over.

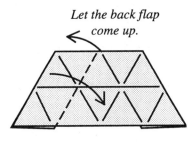

Let the back flap
come up.

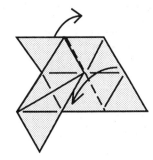

22) Fold along the indicated crease, **but** allow the flap from the back to come up.

23) Repeat step 22 on the right.

24) Unfold steps 22 and 23.

3-D, step 25 in progress...

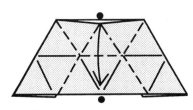

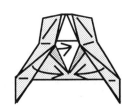

25) Refold steps 22 and 23 simultaneously, **but this time** pull one layer of paper from the top down...

26) ...in this way. Let the left side slip under the right.

27) There. Tuck the flap behind. Rotate 90°.

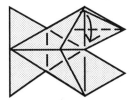

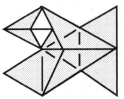

28) Fold one layer down to make the eye.

29) Bingo! Folding the lower flap in step 28 will produce a mirror-image Fish.

Fishy Combinations

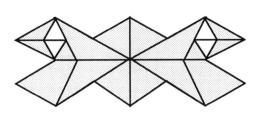

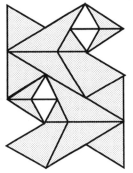

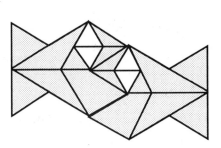

Backed Up

Stacked Up

Each One Eat One

87

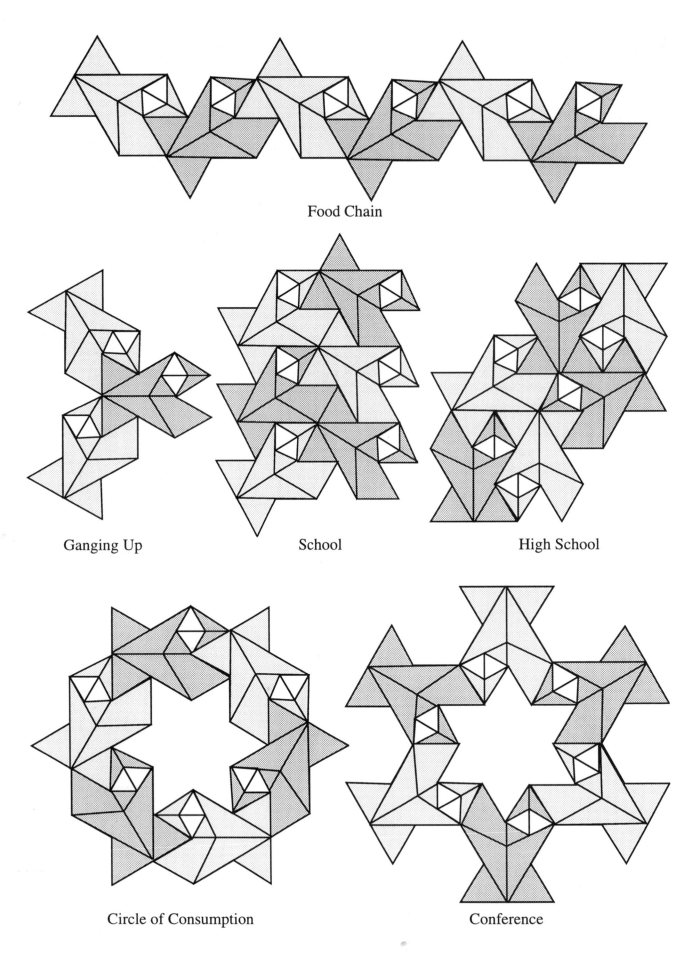

Food Chain

Ganging Up

School

High School

Circle of Consumption

Conference

88

Elephant Major

And now, the most dignified and challenging fold in the book.

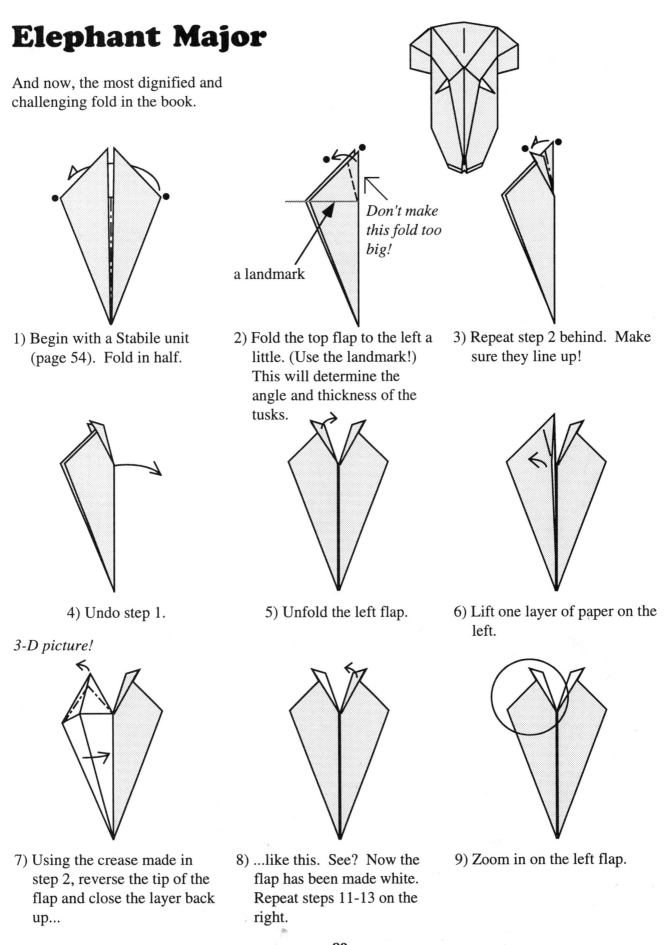

a landmark

Don't make this fold too big!

1) Begin with a Stabile unit (page 54). Fold in half.

2) Fold the top flap to the left a little. (Use the landmark!) This will determine the angle and thickness of the tusks.

3) Repeat step 2 behind. Make sure they line up!

4) Undo step 1.

5) Unfold the left flap.

6) Lift one layer of paper on the left.

3-D picture!

7) Using the crease made in step 2, reverse the tip of the flap and close the layer back up...

8) ...like this. See? Now the flap has been made white. Repeat steps 11-13 on the right.

9) Zoom in on the left flap.

89

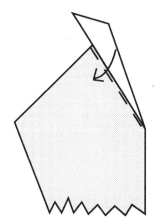 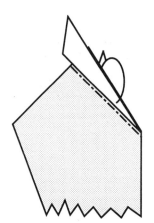 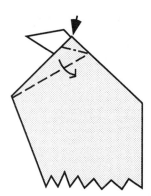

10) Fold along the flap's edge.

11) Fold again along the edge, but this time **away from you**.

12) Tricky: fold the colored edge in a little and flatten the indicated point...

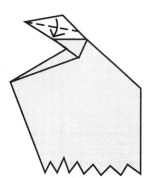 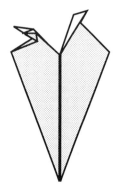 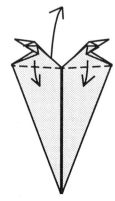

13) ...like this. Fold the tip of the tusk in half.

14) Normal view. **Repeat** steps 10-13 on the right.

15) Fold the two flaps down **and** allow the rear flap to come up.

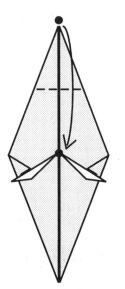 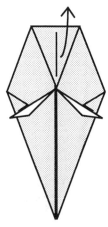 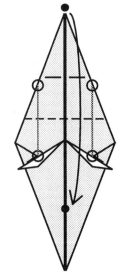

16) Fold the top point to the center.

17) Unfold step 16.

18) Fold the top point down again so that the sides line up with the tusks.

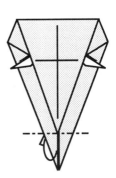
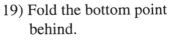

19) Fold the bottom point behind.

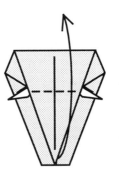

20) Fold the trunk up along the **existing** crease.

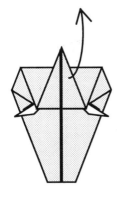

21) Unfold the trunk.

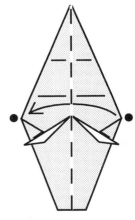

22) Fold in half.

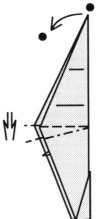

23) Pivot the top point to the left by making "crimps" in the front and back of the middle...

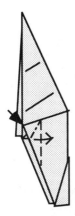

24) ...like this. Bring the left edge to the right by flattening the indicated point...

25) ...like this. The size of this fold will determine how thin or fat the elephant is. Repeat step 24 behind.

Make the crease at this point.

26) Fold the top point down along the left edge as shown.

27) Now unfold steps 22-26 (be brave).

91

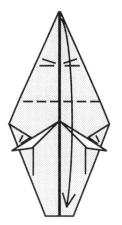 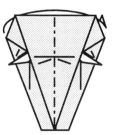 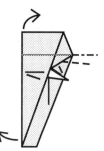

28) Fold the top point down along the existing crease.

29) Fold in half away from you.

30) Now redo the "crimp" fold from step 23.

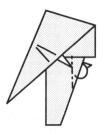 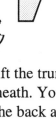  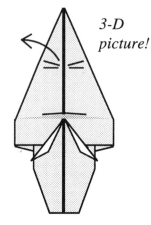

3-D picture!

31) Refold steps 24-25 inside (front and back).

32) Now lift the trunk and peek underneath. You'll have to open the back a little.

33) All right. Lift **one layer of paper** to the left.

  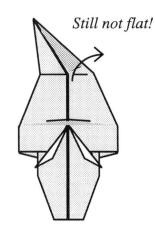

Still not flat!

34) **Follow these creases carefully!** Bring the long, straight crease over the two shorter ones.

35) Then close the left side back up. The top point should bend to the left...

36) ...like this. Repeat steps 33-35 on the right.

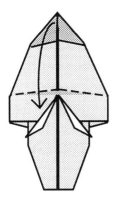  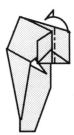

37) Bring the trunk back down and return to the position of step 32.

38) Fold one ear to the left. The paper will be thick, but be persistent.

39) Repeat step 38 behind.

40) Push the bottom left corner in, extending the fold up under the trunk. This will create the illusion of two legs.

41) Unfold the ears and open the back.

42) Flatten the head. Make creases to give the impression of toes (optional).

43) The completed Elephant Major! Congratulations!

Notice that things like the angle of the tusks and the thickness of the legs are all adjustable. Modify steps 2 and 23-25 to make different types of elephants.

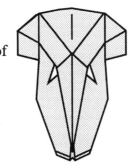

Different trunks may be made as well. Try omitting steps 16, 17, 20, 26, and 32-37. Then, as the final step, try making the trunk shown here. People who have mastered everything else in the book should find this an interesting challenge.

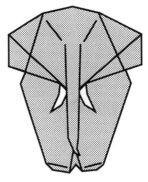

Acknowledgments

One of the most important components in the creation of an origami book is the "testing" phase. Scores of innocent, helpless, and trusting souls must be subjected to the dreadful ROUGH DRAFT. These are the fighters who must struggle through the early diagrams that are "obviously clear" to the author. These are the explorers who must face every error, blunder, oversight, and typo with the word, "Huh?" These are the victims who just happened to be around when the author walked by with sheaves of virgin diagrams, fresh from the laser printer.

In any case, much is owed to them. It is safe to say that any flaws in this book are the fault of the authors, and any positive features are probably due to suggestions from the following people: Mary Beth Abel, Kristen Brennan, Melissa Cahoon, Pasha Dritt, Joanie Franzino, Emily Juda, Karl Kassler, Nancy Marshall, Brenda Rivera, Shira Robbins, Judith Ross-McNab, Beth Nixon, Jan Polish, Fiona Smith, Sarah Smith, Caitlin Strom, Tracy Tshudy, and Amy Weiss.

Special thanks go to our photographer, Lionel Delevingne, who was introduced to origami the hard way. As innocent as it seems, a folded piece of paper can be as photogenic as a pile of mud. Some paper models warp, collect dust, and respond to light in conflicting ways. And some frogs look like flowers when viewed through the lens of a camera. Lionel's concern for aesthetic values, and patience in the face of repeated folding and photographing, was admirable.

We would also like to thank Sam Randlett for the swell copyediting job. Finally, much praise is deserved by our editor, Barbara Anderson, and her assistant, Marian Lizzi, for their kind advice, assistance, and support. If we ever decide to do this again, they'll be the first ones we call.

About the Authors

Bob Neale, in addition to what is mentioned in the introduction, is a free-lance writer and magician, who previously taught for twenty-four years as Professor of Psychiatry and Religion at Union Theological Seminary in New York. He is the author of numerous books and essays on psychology and religion. His current focus is on the psychology of the trickster tradition in religion. Bob has also contributed to many of conjuring's most respected journals, and is the author of a book for magicians, *Tricks of the Imagination.* Not surprisingly, he is noted for the invention of tricks and puzzles that involve folding.

Tom Hull is currently pursuing a Ph.D. in mathematics at the University of Rhode Island, where his studies include complex dynamics, fractals, graph theory, and the relationship between origami and math. He has been exploring origami for fifteen years, and his models and diagrams have appeared in American and international origami journals. Among Tom's other interests are music, Frisbee, dance, and supernatural horror.

List of Symbols

– – – – –   Valley fold

—·—·—·—   Mountain fold

Fold in front

Fold behind

Fold and unfold

Fold this to that

Turn over

Zoom in here (i.e., close-up)

Pinch (hold) here

Open the paper here

Open and flatten (see what the next picture looks like)

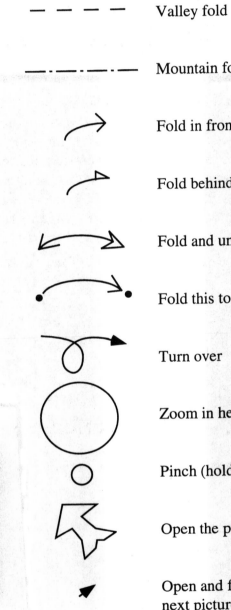